Pronounce It
PERFECTLY
in
ENGLISH

Third Edition

Jean Yates, Ph.D.
American University

BARRON'S

Acknowledgement: The quotation from MY FAIR LADY on page 40, by permission of the Estate of Alan Jay Lerner © 1956 by Alan Jay Lerner and Frederick Loewe.

All inquiries should be addressed to:
Barron's Educational Series, Inc.
250 Wireless Boulevard
Hauppauge, NY 11788
www.barronseduc.com

ISBN: 978-1-4380-7280-7 (book and CD package)
Library of Congress Control Number: 2012945310

Printed in the United States of America
9 8 7 6 5 4 3 2 1

CONTENTS

Introduction   v

PART ONE: English Vowel Sounds

Unit

1	The Sound /ə/	3
2	The Sound /ɪ/	7
3	The Sound /u/	9
4	The Sound /iy/	11
5	The Sound /uw/	15
6	The Sound /iuw/	18
7	The Sound /ʌ/	21
8	The Sound /ɛ/	24
9	The Sound /ow/	28
10	The Sound /oiy/	32
11	The Sound /eə/	34
12	The Sound /eiy/	39
13	The Sound /ɔ/	42
14	The Sound /æ/	46
15	The Sound /æow/	50
16	The Sound /a/	52
17	The Sound /aiy/	56

PART TWO: English Consonant Sounds

18	The Sounds /p/, /b/	61
19	The Sounds /t/, /d/	67
20	The Sounds /k/, /g/	77
21	The Sounds /f/, /v/	84
22	The Sounds /ch/, /j/	90
23	The Sounds /sh/, /zh/	94
24	The Sounds /s/, /z/	98
25	The Sounds /l/, /r/	109
26	The Sounds /m/, /n/, /ŋ/	116
27	The Sounds /θ/, /ð/	127
28	The Sound /h/	133
29	The Sounds /w/, /y/	135
30	Double Consonants	141

Part Three: Stress Patterns

31	Syllables and Stress	145
32	Two-Syllable Words	146
33	Words with Three or More Syllables	154
34	One-Syllable Prefixes	159
35	Two-Syllable Prefixes	161
36	Suffixes	163
37	Sentence Stress	168

Part Four: Intonation Patterns

38	Greetings	181
39	Statements	182
40	Questions	183
41	Counting and Listing	186
42	Options	187

Part Five: Appendix

| 1 | More Words to Practice | 189 |
| 2 | Pronunciation Differences When the Letter *e* Is Added to a One-Syllable Word | 196 |

INTRODUCTION

The goal of "perfect pronunciation" is not to take your personality out of your speech. Indeed, mannerisms that give hints of your origin are charming in English. The goal is, rather, to speak so that people listen to *what* you say, not *how* you say it. The goal is to be understood the first time you say something, and to be confident and proud of the way you speak.

This book and four CDs are designed to help you pronounce English words, phrases, and sentences correctly, so that the meaning you intend is clear and the sounds are pleasing to the ear.

The materials are organized to help you get through the maze of English spelling so that you will know how to pronounce any new word. English spelling reflects the history of the words rather than how they are pronounced. The spelling of the vowel sounds, in particular, is an unreliable guide to their pronunciation. Also, many vowel and consonant letters are silent: they are simply not pronounced at all. Most importantly, however, the pronunciation of many grammatical markers systematically changes according to the sounds that precede them, and these changes are not reflected in the spelling. Native speakers do not even notice these changes, but make them automatically. You will learn to do the same thing.

The book is divided into five parts: Vowel Sounds, Consonant Sounds, Stress Patterns, Intonation Patterns, and Appendix. Each sound is considered separately, by sound rather than by spelling. There are instructions and diagrams to show you how the sound is made. Examples are given of the sound in all possible positions in a word or phrase, and examples are given of all possible spellings of the sound. The unique stress and intonation patterns of English, which often carry meaning, are described in detail, with examples for practice. The CDs include all of these examples, modeled by native speakers, with pauses provided so that you can repeat them.

The book and CDs also include exercises, quizzes, and practice materials to help you make sure you are hearing and producing the sounds correctly.

As the pronunciation of grammatical markers is vital for understanding, there are sections entitled "Usage Tips" throughout the materials. Pay particular attention to these sections. If you are a beginner, or have trouble making yourself understood, do these sections first, and continue to practice them.

Do not be discouraged if at first you do not hear the differences in sounds. You can train yourself to hear them. Follow the instructions for making the sounds; check yourself by looking in the mirror; tape-record your voice. Practice making the differences and you will begin to hear them.

The book and CDs are coordinated so that you can use them separately or together. To improve your understanding of English spelling and your recognition of written words, listen to the CDs while looking at the words and sentences in the book. When you listen to the recording without the book, simply repeat the examples during the pauses provided for writing, and do the written exercises later.

The symbols used to represent each sound are based on those of the International Phonetic Alphabet. Because many English vowel sounds are combinations of sounds, they are represented here by combinations of symbols. This is intended to help the learner form these sounds by combining their individual parts.

The pronunciation symbols used by *The American Heritage Dictionary, The Random House Dictionary, The Merriam-Webster Dictionary, The Oxford Dictionary,* and *Longman's Dictionary* appear on page vii, so that you may use this book as a pronunciation guide for any new word you look up in your own dictionary.

Guide to Symbols

Unit	Barron's	Longman's	Oxford	Random House	American Heritage	Merriam Webster
1	ə	ə	e o i a u	ə	ə	ə
2	ɪ	ɪ	ĭ	i	ĭ	i
3	u	ʊ	o͞o	o͞o	o͞o	u̇
4	iy	iʸ	ē	e	ē	ē
5	uw	uʷ	o͞o	o͞o	o͞o	ü
6	iuw	ju	ū	yo͞o	iu	yü
7	ʌ	ʌ	ŭ	u	ŭ	ˈə
8	ɛ	e	ĕ	e	ĕ	e
9	ow	əʊ	ō	ō	ō	ō
10	oiy	ɔɪ	oi	oi	oi	ȯi
11	eə	eə	ë	â	â	a
12	eiy	eɪ	ā	ā	ā	ā
13	ɔ	ɔ	aw	ô	ô	ȯ
14	æ	æ	ă	a	ă	a
15	æow	aʊ	ow	ou	ou	au̇
16	a	a	ah	ä	ŏ	ä
17	aiy	aɪ	ī	ī	ī	ī
18	p b	p b	p b	p b	p b	p b
19	t d	t d	t d	t d	t d	t d
20	k g	k g	k g	k g	k g	k g
21	f v	f v	f v	f v	f v	f v
22	ch j	tʃ dʒ	ch j	ch j	ch j	ch j
23	sh zh	ʃ ʒ	sh zh	sh zh	sh zh	sh zh
24	s z .	s z	s z	s z	s z	s z
25	l r	l r	l r	l r	l r	l r
26	m n ŋ	m n ŋ	m n ng	m n ng	m n ng	m n ŋ
27	θ ð	θ ð	th dh	th th	th t͟h	th t͟h
28	h	h	h	h	h	h
29	w y	w j	w y	w y	w y	w y

PART ONE
English Vowel Sounds

Every vowel sound represents a syllable in a word.

Syllables are either emphasized and "stressed," or weak and "unstressed."

There are 17 different vowel sounds in English.

They all have "voice," which occurs as the vocal cords vibrate.

The tongue does not touch other parts of the mouth, teeth, or lips.

The vowel sounds differ by

- the distance between the lips
- the shape of the lips
- the position of the tongue
- the length of time the sound is held

The vowel sounds are ordered in this book according to how open the mouth is. The first sound, /ə/, is made with the mouth almost closed. As the lessons progress, the mouth gradually opens. The final sound, /**aiy**/, is made with the mouth wide open.

There are three tongue positions:

high – the tongue is close to the palate, but does not touch it
mid – the tongue is in the center, level with the edges of the
        top teeth
low – the tongue rests behind the bottom teeth

To pronounce each vowel correctly, follow these steps:

- Look in the mirror.
- Compare your mouth with each diagram.
- Make short sounds quickly.
- Count to two, silently, for long sounds.

Every vowel sound in English has more than one spelling. In each vowel unit you will find a chart that details every possible spelling of the featured sound and gives numerous examples of each spelling. Where there are only three or fewer words listed, these are the only common words that feature this spelling.

Unit One
The Sound /ə/

Introducing the Sound

We begin with the vowel sound /ə/ for several reasons:

* it is the most common vowel sound in English; most words of more than one syllable contain this sound in the softer, or *unstressed*, syllable,
* many one-syllable words are pronounced with this sound,
* it can be spelled with any of the five vowel letters, and also with combinations of letters,
* it is an important sound for certain grammatical markers (see pages 73, 105, 146),
* native speakers automatically know when to pronounce this sound, without being told why or in what circumstances,
* pronouncing this vowel sound correctly is one of the most important skills necessary for clear communication.

The sound /ə/ is easy to pronounce. To make it, simply open your mouth very slightly, and make a noise. It does not sound like a formed vowel, and it isn't. The lips and tongue are relaxed, and the voice makes a short, soft noise. (See Figure 1.)

/ə/ in Unstressed Syllables

Figure 1.
The sound /ə/

However, it takes a lot of practice to know when to use this sound. As it can be spelled in so many different ways, we have printed in *light blue italics* the letters that are pronounced with this sound in the Examples and Exercise sections throughout this book. This will identify the sound while preserving the correct spelling of the words. When you see a vowel identified this way, pronounce it as softly and as quickly as you can, giving it no emphasis.

Listen to the following examples of words with the sound /ə/ in unstressed syllables and repeat them after the speaker.

EXAMPLES

/ə/ in first syllable	/ə/ in second syllable		/ə/ in other syllables
a-go	so-d*a*	cap-t*ai*n	*o*-ca-s*io*n-*a*l-ly
*e*f-fect	o-p*en*	pi-g*eo*n	g*a*-ra-g*e*s
*e*x-plain	den-*i*m	par-t*ia*l	poi-s*o*n-*ou*s
*o*c-cur	meth-*o*d	sta-t*io*n	pan-*o*-ra-m*a*
u-pon	syr-*u*p	cup-b*oa*rd	u-n*i*-ver-s*a*l

In addition to being spelled by all the vowel letters and combinations of letters, the /ə/ sound can also be pronounced when there is no vowel at all. Listen to the following examples, and repeat them after the speaker.

EXAMPLES

prism	(pris-əm)
socialism	(so-c*ial*-is-əm)
nationalism	(na-t*ion*-*al*-is-əm)

In certain contractions (see also pages 119, 120), the /ə/ sound is pronounced at the same time as the /**n**/ sound. Listen to the following examples, and repeat them after the speaker.

EXAMPLES

doesn't	(does-ənt)
isn't	(is-ənt)
hasn't	(has-ənt)
wasn't	(was-ənt)
haven't	(hav-ənt)
didn't	(did-ənt)
hadn't	(had-ənt)
shouldn't	(should-ənt)
wouldn't	(would-ənt)
couldn't	(could-ənt)

The consonant-vowel sequence <u>le</u>, especially at the end of a word, is usually pronounced əl. Listen to the following examples, and repeat them after the speaker.

EXAMPLES

abl*e*	(a-bəl)
cap*a*bl*e*	(cap-*a*-bəl)
suit*a*bl*e*	(suit-*a*-bəl

Usage Tip

- The words <u>a</u>, <u>an</u>, and <u>the</u> are articles, unstressed words that occur before nouns and adjective-noun combinations. Say them quickly, without emphasis. Pronounce the vowel as /ə/.

Listen to the following examples of articles containing the /ə/ sound, and repeat them after the speaker.

EXAMPLES

a book	*a*n appl*e* (pəl)	th*e* book
a cat	*a*n or*a*nge	th*e* cat
a dog	*a*n ice cube	th*e* dog
		th*e* un*i*verse

(When <u>the</u> occurs before a word beginning with a vowel sound, the <u>e</u> is pronounced /**iy**/. (See Unit Four, page 11.)

/ə/ in Stressed Syllables

When /ə/ is followed by the consonant /**r**/, it can be the prominent, or *stressed* vowel of a word. In the examples that follow, and throughout the rest of this book, the sound that is being introduced will be printed in **boldface** type.

The tongue is in mid position for this sound.

Listen to the examples and repeat them after the speaker.

EXAMPLES

ur	er	ear	ir	or	our	yr	olo
urn **fur** **pur**se	s**er**ve n**er**ve	**ear**n h**ear**d y**ear**ns	b**ir**d g**ir**l f**ir**st	w**or**k w**or**m	t**our**nament	s**yr**up	
b**ur**n ch**ur**ch f**ur**nish p**ur**ple sp**ur**t t**ur**n	b**er**th c**er**tain c**er**tify h**er**b m**er**cy s**er**vice v**er**b	**ear**th d**ear**th l**ear**n s**ear**ch	b**ir**th d**ir**ty m**ir**th s**ir** v**ir**tue z**ir**con	w**or**d w**or**ry w**or**se w**or**ship w**or**st w**or**th	n**our**ish j**our**ney fl**our**ish c**our**age	s**yr**inge	col**o**nel

Practice for Mastery

Listen to the following sentences that feature the sound /ə/, and repeat them after the speaker.

EXAMPLES

> I h**ear**d h**er** j**our**ney w*a*s w**or**th th*e* w**or**ry.
> Th*e* sug*a*r w*a*s th*e* col*o*r of **ear**th.
> The **ear**ly b**ir**d gets th*e* w**or**m.

Continue to practice this sound while learning the rest of the vowel sounds. Remember that the /ə/ sound will be written in *blue italics* when it occurs in unstressed syllables.

UNIT TWO
THE SOUND /ɪ/

Introducing the Sound

To make the /ɪ/ sound, lower your jaw slightly. The lips are relaxed and are about ¼ inch (6 mm) apart. (See Figure 2.)

The tongue is high.

The sound is short.

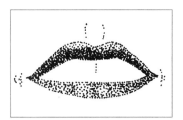

Figure 2.
The sound /ɪ/

Listen to the examples and repeat them after the speaker.

EXAMPLES

i	*ui*	*y*	*e*	*ie*	*u*	*o*
if in big miss	build	gym symbol	pretty English	sieve	busy	women
bit city ditch finish give pig rich silver will quilt	built guild guilt	lyrics tyranny			business	

Practice for Mastery

Listen to the following sentences featuring the vowel sound /ɪ/ and repeat them after the speaker.

EXAMPLES

Jim is in the picture.
Miss Smith is thin.
Bring chicken for dinner.
Listen to this ridiculous list.
The pretty women are busy in the gym.

UNIT THREE
The Sound /u/

Introducing the Sound

This vowel is formed by keeping the jaw slightly open. The lips are ¼ inch (6 mm) apart and pushed outward to make an open circle. (See Figure 3.)

The tongue is in mid position.

The sound is short.

Figure 3.
The sound /u/

Listen to the examples and repeat them after the speaker.

EXAMPLES

u	*oo*	*oul*	*o*
put push	look book	could would	woman wolf
bush bushel cushion pudding	cook crooked hood nook rook shook took	should	

Practice for Mastery

Listen to the following sentences featuring the sound /**u**/, and repeat them after the speaker.

EXAMPLES

> L**oo**k in th*e* c**oo**kb**oo**k f*o*r *a* g**oo**d p**u**dding.
> He w**ou**ld if he c**ou**ld.
> It sh**ou**ld be g**oo**d w**oo**l.
> Th*e* wom*a*n t**oo**k *a* g**oo**d l**oo**k *a*t the w**o**lf.

UNIT FOUR
The Sound /iy/

Introducing the Sound

To make this sound, set your lips ⅜ inch (1 cm) apart. Widen your lips into a big smile. (See Figure 4.)

The tongue is in mid position.

The sound is long. Count to two silently to be sure it is long enough.

Figure 4.
The sound /iy/

Listen to the following examples and repeat them after the speaker.

EXAMPLES

e	ee	y	ey	ea	eo
be he we	bee see sweet	marry happy	key honey	cheap fear	people
decent deny evil hero mere recede recent here	beer feeble feel feet freeze gee knee leeway need queen tee wee	bully crazy dizzy gaudy happy jazzy nearly pretty really silly timely ugly very	money	bean cheat crease ease feasible grease hear heat jeans lease meal peach season tease	

oe	ei	ie	i	Is	ois
*a*moeb*a*	either receive	niece	ski police suite	chassis debris	chamois
	conceive deceive neither receive weird	fierce lien piece piedmont pierce	chemise		

Usage Tips

- The e in the article the is pronounced /**iy**/ when it is followed by a word beginning with a vowel sound.

Listen to the examples and repeat them after the speaker.

EXAMPLES

the apple	the orange	the ocean
the elephant	the onion	the umpire
the ice		

- The /**iy**/ sound, spelled y at the end of a word often indicates an adjective.

Listen to the examples and repeat them after the speaker.

EXAMPLES

tricky	soapy	sticky	heavy
edgy	chilly	shaky	**easy**

- Adverbs often end in the syllable ly, pronounced /**liy**/.

Listen to the examples and repeat them after the speaker.

EXAMPLES

nicely	quickly	slowly
plainly	sweetly	clearly

- A final /**iy**/ sound after a name can indicate endearment or informality.

Listen to the examples and repeat them after the speaker.

EXAMPLES

sw**ee**tie	S**u**sie	dadd**y**
Bobb**y**	momm**y**	cut**ie**

Practice for Mastery

Listen to the following sentences featuring the vowel sound /**iy**/ and repeat them after the speaker.

EXAMPLES

Jeannie, do you **s**ee the **b**ees?
Please freeze the peas.
Neither he nor she believes me.
We can easily read the agreement.

Contrasting Sound Practice

Compare the sound /ɪ/ from Unit Two with the sound /**iy**/, by repeating the following words after the speaker.

EXAMPLES

/ɪ/	/iy/	/ɪ/	/iy/
bit	beet	rich	reach
sit	seat	pick	peak, peek
rip	reap	dim	deem
lip	leap	dip	deep
live	leave	sin	seen, scene
did	deed	fist	feast
hill	heel, heal, he'll	sis	cease
mill	meal	his	he's
pill	peel, peal	ship	sheep
lick	leak, leek	chip	cheap

Now listen to several sentences that feature both sounds, and repeat them after the speaker.

> Six sheep were sick on the ship.
> Jim eats cheap chips.
> He leaves me this measly little meal.
> She's as thin as he is.
> Please peel the beets and string the beans.

Recognition Practice

The speaker will pronounce five words featuring these sounds. During the pauses, circle the word you hear. If it is not convenient for you to write at this time, use the pauses to repeat the words after the speaker, then complete the written exercise later. The correct answers appear below.

EXERCISE

1. sin	scene
2. live	leave
3. his	he's
4. hill	he'll
5. sit	seat

Dictation Practice

Now the speaker will pronounce five words featuring these two sounds. During the pauses, write each word on a piece of paper. If it is not convenient for you to write at this time, use the pauses to repeat the words after the speaker, then complete the written exercise later. The correct answers appear below.

Answers to Exercises

Recognition Practice, scene, live, his, he'll, seat

Dictation Practice, dip, meal, reach, sin, he's

Unit Five
The Sound /uw/

Introducing the Sound

To make the /**uw**/ sound, keep the mouth slightly open and the lips ⅜ inch (1 cm) apart. The lips are tense, and pushed forward into a small circle. (See Figure 5.)

The tongue is in mid position.

The sound is long.

Figure 5.
The sound /uw/

Listen to the examples and repeat them after the speaker.

EXAMPLES

o	*oe*	*oo*	*ough*	*ou*	*u*
do lose who two	canoe shoe	loose choose food	through	soup	Flu rude
move movie prove to		coo cool loop room school zoo		bouquet boutique routine souvenir	duke junior ludicrous nude spruce

15

ui	ue	eu	ew	ieu	oup
juice	due blue Tuesday	rheumatism	flew new	lieu	
nuisance	avenue rue sue		dew Jewish lewd stewed	lieutenant	coup

Practice for Mastery

Listen to the following sentences featuring the sound /**uw**/ and repeat them after the speaker.

EXAMPLES

> **Sue** knew th**e** truth.
> Choose blue for th**e** new room.
> It blooms soon, in June.
> Th**e** news **is** too gloomy.

Contrasting Sound Practice

Now compare the sound /**u**/ from Unit Three with the sound /**uw**/. Listen and repeat each word after the speaker.

EXAMPLES

/**u**/	/**uw**/	/**u**/	/**uw**/
full	fool	pull	pool
stood	stewed	cookie	kooky
would, wood	wooed	nook	nuke
hood	who'd		

Now repeat the following sentences, which feature both vowel sounds.

EXAMPLES

> Lou couldn't fool Sue.
> Stu wouldn't move th**e** cooking school.
> Th**e** good pool room is booked for Tuesday **a**t noon.
> Th**e** cook stood **a**nd looked **a**t his new shoes.

Recognition Practice

The speaker will pronounce five words. In your book, circle the ones you hear, or repeat them now and do the written exercise later. The correct answers appear below.

Exercise

1. hood	who'd
2. full	fool
3. wood	wooed
4. nook	nuke
5. stood	stewed

Dictation Practice

Write the next five words recorded on the CD on a piece of paper, or repeat them during the pauses and write the exercise later. The correct answers appear below.

Keep in mind that learning to make the sounds correctly and practicing them will help you to hear their differences.

Spelling Challenge

Four sentences containing words with tricky spelling are next recorded on the CD. Write them down during the pauses, then check your work below. If it is not convenient for you to write at this time, repeat the sentences during the pauses, and write them later.

Answers to Exercises

Recognition Practice, hood, full, wooed, nook, stewed

Dictation Practice, who'd, stood, pool, would, full

Spelling Challenge, I see a big woman and two little women.

We drank sweet juice in the hotel suite. It's good food.

Don't shoot him in the foot.

Unit Six
The Sound /iuw/

Introducing the Sound

The /**iuw**/ sound is a combination of the sounds /**iy**/ and /**uw**/. The lips are ⅜ inch (1 cm) apart. Begin with the lips spread into a big smile, then push them forward into a circle. (See Figure 6.)

The tongue is low, then rises to mid position.

The sound is short.

Figure 6.
The sound /iuw/

Listen to the examples and repeat them after the speaker.

EXAMPLES

u	ew	ie	eu	eau	ou	ue
use cute music	yew few ewe	view	feud	beauty	you	hue
*a*ccuse fu*e*l fugue	hew					cue queue

The Sound /iə/

When /**iuw**/ occurs in unstressed syllables, the second sound of the combination changes from /**uw**/ to /**ə**/. Begin with the lips ⅜ inch apart, and make the /**iy**/ sound. Move the lips to the almost-closed and relaxed position of /**ə**/.

18

The tongue remains in mid position.

Listen to the examples and repeat them after the speaker.

EXAMPLES

u	*iu*	*io*	*ua*	*yo*
imm*u*nize	med*iu*m	un*io*n	us*ua*lly	can*yo*n

The Sound /iə/ + r

EXAMPLES

*u*r	*you*r	*eu*r
acc*u*rate	*you*r	*Eu*rope
fail*u*re		*Eu*rope*a*n
fig*u*re		
*U*ral		
*U*ran*u*s		
*u*rine		

Usage Tip

The article <u>a</u> is used before words that begin with a consonant sound, while <u>an</u> is used before those that begin with a vowel sound. While <u>u</u> and <u>eu</u> are vowels, when they are pronounced /**iuw**/, they actually begin with the consonant sound /**y**/ (see page 137). For this reason, use the article <u>a</u> (pronounced /ə/) instead of <u>an</u> before words beginning with /**iuw**/.

Listen to the examples, and repeat them after the speaker.

EXAMPLES

<u>u</u> pronounced as a vowel
*a*n umbrell*a*
*a*n understanding
*a*n understatement
*a*n ugly situat*i*on
*a*n unusu*a*l occurre*n*ce

u pronounced as /**iuw**/
a **un**ion
a **u**se
a **u**sef*u*l gadg*e*t
a **u**til*i*ty
a **u**su*a*l *o*ccurrence
eu pronounced as /**iuw**/
a **eu**phoric sensat*i*on
a **eu**ph*e*mism (is*ə*m)
a **eu**l*o*gy
a **Eu**r*o*pean

EXAMPLES

This is *a* **u**nivers*a*l truth.
It is *a* **un**iver*s*ity in New York.
They w*i*ll form *a* **u**ni*o*n.
This *is a* **u**su*a*l *o*ccurrence.

Practice for Mastery

Listen to the following sentences featuring the sound /**iuw**/, and repeat them after the speaker.

EXAMPLES

A **few** beau*ti*es w*e*re in th*e* pic*tu*re.
Your **cu**es *a*re c*o*nfus*i*ng.
He w*a*s *a*ccused *o*f *a*buse.
Are **you** **u**sed t*o* **u**sing th*e* c*o*mpu*te*r?

UNIT SEVEN
THE SOUND /ʌ/

Introducing the Sound

To make this sound, keep the mouth slightly open, with lips about ⅜ inch (1 cm) apart. (See Figure 7.)

The tongue is in low position.

The sound is short.

Figure 7.
The sound /ʌ/

Listen to the following examples and repeat them after the speaker.

EXAMPLES

u	*o*	*ou*	*oo*	*oe*	*a*
up under	love done son	cousin trouble rough	flood blood	does	was
bump crumb fun gusto jump luck lust mud puppy rust sun trust	dove front honey money nothing some wonder				wasn't

Practice for Mastery

Listen to the following sentences featuring the sound /ʌ/ and repeat them after the speaker.

EXAMPLES

> Buffy cut up the shrubs.
> The dust is under the rug.
> The mother won some of the money, but not enough.
> I'd love to come on Sunday if it's sunny.

Contrasting Sound Practice

To compare the /u/ from Unit Three with the sound /ʌ/, listen to the following words and repeat them after the speaker.

EXAMPLES

/u/	/ʌ/	/u/	/ʌ/
took	tuck	put	putt
look	luck	could	cud
book	buck		

Now listen to sentences that feature both vowel sounds, and repeat them after the speaker.

EXAMPLES

> Could you put a tuck in the front?
> Look at us for good luck.
> The bus looks good, but it's fun on foot.
> The hooded one looks tough.

Recognition Practice

Five words featuring these sounds are recorded on the CD. Circle below the words you hear. The correct answers are below.

EXERCISE

1. look   luck
2. took   tuck
3. put   putt
4. could   cud
5. put   putt

Dictation Practice

Write the next five words recorded on the CD on a piece of paper, or repeat them during the pauses and write the exercise later. The correct answers appear below.

Spelling Challenge

Three sentences that have words with tricky spelling are next recorded on the CD. Listen to each one carefully, then write it down during the pause. Check your sentences below.

Answers to Exercises

Recognition Practice, luck, took, putt, could, put

Dictation Practice, luck, took, book, could, buck

Spelling Challenge, Stop rushing and pushing. The bus is busy.

The poodle stood in a puddle of blood.

Unit Eight
The Sound /ɛ/

Introducing the Sound

To make this sound, lower your jaw slightly. The lips are tense and spread outward in a half-smile, about ½ inch (1.3 cm) apart. (See Figure 8.)

The tongue is in low position.

The sound is short.

Figure 8.
The sound /ɛ/

Listen to the following examples and repeat them after the speaker.

EXAMPLES

e	a	ai	ay	ea	eo
egg edge step	any many can	*a*gain said	says	meadow head	 leop*a*rd
led cell felt jelly left men next quest rel*a*tive secti*o*n when				dead jeal*ou*s lead (metal) meant pleas*a*nt meas*u*re treas*u*re weather zeal*ou*s	jeop*a*rdy

24

ie	*ei*	*ue*	*u*	*ee*
friend	heifer	guest	bury	been
		guess		

Practice for Mastery

Listen to the following sentences featuring the sound /ɛ/ and repeat them after the speaker.

EXAMPLES

> Send Ben for his friend.
> Let's rent a tent.
> Esther never gets upset.
> Fred said it again and again.

Contrasting Sound Practice

To compare the /ɪ/ sound from Unit Two with the sound /ɛ/, listen to these words and repeat them after the speaker.

EXAMPLES

/ɪ/	/ɛ/	/ɪ/	/ɛ/
pick	peck	fill	fell
bid	bed	gym	gem
lid	led, lead	tin	ten
miss	mess	slipped	slept
wrist	rest	mitt	met
lift	left	six	sex
big	beg		

Now repeat the following sentences which feature both vowel sounds.

EXAMPLES

> Pick a peck of pickled peppers.
> Ed slipped and fell in the gym.
> Evelyn missed the best bid.
> Peg slept from six 'til ten, then left.

Recognition Practice

Five words featuring these sounds are recorded on the CD. Circle below the words you hear, then check them on page 27.

EXERCISE

1. lid   led
2. big   beg
3. slipped   slept
4. gym   gem
5. lift   left

Dictation Practice

Five words that contain these sounds are recorded on the CD. Write them during the pauses, then check them on page 27.

If you do not hear the difference between the two vowel sounds, do not be discouraged. By making the sounds correctly, putting your lips and jaw in the positions described, you will begin to hear the difference.

Spelling Challenge

Three sentences containing words with tricky spelling are recorded next on the CD. During the pauses, write them down on a piece of paper. Check them on page 27.

Now compare /iy/ from Unit Four with the sound /ɛ/. Listen to the examples and repeat them after the speaker.

EXAMPLES

/iy/	/ɛ/	/iy/	/ɛ/
beat, beet	bet	read, reed	red, read
feel	fell	seed	said
geese	guess	sealing, ceiling	selling
he'd, heed	head	sees	says
mean	men	bleed	bled

Listen to several sentences that feature these two sounds, and repeat them after the speaker.

EXAMPLES

> Please feed the pets and weed the beds.
> He said he'd eat the red meat.
> She says she fell and she's bleeding.
> Steve guessed he'd been seen in the shed.

Recognition Practice

Five words featuring these sounds are recorded next on the CD. Circle below the ones you hear. The correct answers appear below.

EXERCISE

1. teen	ten
2. mean	men
3. heed	head
4. seal	sell
5. geese	guess

Dictation Practice

Now the speaker will pronounce five words featuring these sounds. Write the words on a piece of paper, then check your answers with the list below.

Answers to Exercises

Recognition Practice, p. 26 lid, big, slept, gem, left

Dictation Practice, p. 26 tin, miss, pick, bed, six

Spelling Challenge, The queen has been seen. He's the truest guest. Betty is pretty already.

Recognition Practice, ten, mean, head, seal, geese

Dictation Practice, said, wrecks, feel, he'd or heed, guess

Unit Nine
The Sound /ow/

Introducing the Sound

To pronounce /**ow**/, with your lips about ½ inch (1.3 cm) apart, round them into a circle. Begin the sound, then move your lips into a smaller circle. (See Figure 9.)

The tongue is in low position.

The sound is long.

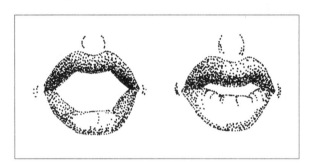

Figure 9.
The sound /ow/

Listen to the examples and repeat them after the speaker.

EXAMPLES

o	eau	ow	eo	oh	ot	ough
over g**o** zer**o**	plat**eau**	**ow**ner sl**ow** wind**ow**	yeo**ma**n	**oh**	dep**o**t	th**ough**
c**o**ld d**o**nate d**o**nut n**o** **o**ver p**o**ny p**o**st s**o**	band**eau** chat**eau**	b**ow** gr**ow** kn**ow** l**ow** m**ow** r**ow** s**ow** t**ow**				d**ough**

oe	oa	ew	ou	o_e	au	oo
hoe	groan	sew	soul shoulder	bone stone	mauve faux	brooch
Joe toe woe	boat coach float gloat groan load loaf loan poach roach roast soap toast		boulder mould	cone cope dope dote grope hope note phone quote vote	taupe	

Practice for Mastery

Listen to the following sentences featuring the sound /**ow**/ and repeat them after the speaker.

EXAMPLES

Oh n**o**, d**o**n't g**o**!
Sh**ow** J**oe** th**e** sn**ow**mobile.
Fl**o** ch**o**se t**o** r**ow** the **o**ld b**oa**t.
Thr**ow** y**ou**r st**o**le **o**ver y**ou**r sh**ou**lder.

The /**ow**/ followed by the consonant /**r**/ is slightly different. When rounding your lips, push them outward, away from the top teeth, making the /**r**/ sound. (See pages 110–111.)

Listen to the examples and repeat them after the speaker.

EXAMPLES

or	ar	our	oor	oar	owar	awer
or for wore	war warm	four pour	poor door	soar board	toward	drawer

chore more nor porch quorum sore tore yore	warden		boor floor moor	hoard roar		

Practice for Mastery

Listen to the following sentences featuring the sound /or/, and repeat them after the speaker.

EXAMPLES

> **Your** war stories *a*re boring.
> He wore shorts t*o* th*e* store.
> **Pour four** more quarts.
> Mort*o*n's court report w*a*s short.

Contrasting Sound Practice

Now compare /ʌ/ from Unit Seven, with /ow/. Listen to the words and repeat them after the speaker.

EXAMPLES

/ʌ/	/ow/	/ʌ/	/ow/
fun	phone	shun	shone
rum	roam	rub	robe
dove	dove	mud	mode, mowed
come	comb	rug	rogue
hum	home	cup	cope
crumb	chrome	nut	note

Now say the following sentences.

> Bud wrote one note home.
> Rose coped with the crumbs.
> Lola rubbed the mud from the old rug.
> Phone him at home just for fun.

Recognition Practice

The speaker will pronounce five words containing these sounds. Circle the words you hear, or repeat them now, and do the written exercise later. The answers are below.

Exercise

1. cup	cope
2. come	comb
3. nut	note
4. fun	phone
5. shun	shone

Dictation Practice

Now write the next five words recorded on the CD on a piece of paper. Check your answers below.

Spelling Challenge

Ten sentences containing words with confusing spelling are recorded next on the tape. Write them down on a piece of paper during the pauses, then check your work below.

Answers to Exercises

Recognition Practice, p. 31 cup, comb, nut, phone, shone

Dictation Practice, p. 31 rug, note, cup, coat, home

Spelling Challenge, Whose shoes are those? Whose hose did you lose? So, sew a few new suits. Move it above the stove. Go do it. Come home. The mover put a cover over the oven. Does she have toes in her shoes? Worms have many forms. Work with the fork.

Unit Ten
The Sound /oiy/

Introducing the Sound

The /**oiy**/ sound is a combination of two sounds beginning with /**o**/ and ending in /**iy**/. The lips, set about ½ inch (1.3 cm) apart, begin in a circle. (See Figure 10.) They move quickly to form a wide smile, ⅜ inch (1 cm) apart.

The tongue is in mid position.

The sound is long.

Figure 10.
The sound /oiy/

Listen to the examples and repeat them after the speaker.

EXAMPLES

oy	oi
boy	boil
toy	soil
	coin
	poise
	noisy
coy	groin
joy	join
loyal	loin
royal	spoil
soy	toil
	voile

Practice for Mastery

Listen to the following sentences featuring the sound /**oiy**/, and repeat them after the speaker.

EXAMPLES

Roy's toys are noisy.
The boy pointed to the poison.
Troy's ploy was foiled.
The spoiled boy destroyed Floyd's joy.

UNIT ELEVEN
THE SOUND /eə/

Introducing the Sound

To make this sound, keep your jaw halfway open. The lips are ½ inch (1.3 cm) apart. Tense your lips, and form a wide, downward smile. Begin the sound, then move your lips close together into the /ə/ position. (See Figure 11.)

The tongue is in mid position.

The sound is long.

Figure 11.
The sound /eə/

Listen to the examples and repeat them after the speaker.

EXAMPLES

a	*au*
ran	laugh
fast	
pass	
craft	
bank	
gas	
half	
sank	
vast	

To pronounce the vowel /eə/ followed by the consonant /r/, begin with the /eə/ sound, then move the lips forward into a round shape, baring the front teeth.

As before, listen to the examples and repeat them after the speaker.

EXAMPLES

are	*ear*	*aer*	*air*	*eir*	*ere*	*ey're*	*ayer*
care dare	wear bear	aerial	fair stairs	heir their	where there	they're	prayer
bare fare hare mare pare rare spare square stare	pear tear	aerate aerie aerobics	hair lair pair				

Practice for Mastery

Repeat the following sentences after the speaker.

EXAMPLES

The fair-haired man ran in the sand.
Where are the spare pairs Stan and Dan wear?
They're not your socks. They're theirs.
Frances laughed when she passed him on the stairs.
They're cramming for their exams over there.

Contrasting Sound Practice

Compare /**iy**/, from Unit Four, with /**eə**/ by repeating the following words.

EXAMPLES

/iy/	/eə/
leaf	laugh
mean	man
clean	clan
fiend	fanned
peace, piece	pass
leaned	land
we're	where, wear
beer	bear
cheer	chair
peer	pear, pair, pare
steer	stair, stare
fear	fair, fare
here, hear	hair, hare
ear	air
tear, tier	tear

Now say these sentences, which feature both vowel sounds.

EXAMPLES

Sheila ran past the stairs with a can of beer.
The lean man cheered and laughed.
She can't eat peas from a can.
We're in need of a tank of gas.

Recognition Practice

The speaker will pronounce five words. Circle the ones you hear, or repeat the words and do the written exercise later. The answers are on page 38.

EXERCISE

1. peace	pass
2. here	hair
3. we're	where
4. leaned	land
5. ear	air

Dictation Practice

Write the next five words recorded on the CD on a piece of paper, then check your work on page 38.

Contrasting Sound Practice

To compare /ɛ/ from Unit Eight with /eə/, repeat the following words after the speaker.

EXAMPLES

/ɛ/	/eə/	/ɛ/	/eə/
lend	land	men	man
left	laughed	messed	mast
pen	pan	guess	gas
wren	ran		

Now repeat several sentences that feature these sounds.

EXAMPLES

The man laughed, then left.
I guess Ann and Ed ran out of gas.
Fran passed the pen to the man's left hand.
Can Ted send a letter to Stan?

Recognition Practice

Listen to the next five words recorded on the CD and circle the ones you hear. The answers are below.

Exercise

1. men   man
2. pen   pan
3. wren   ran
4. lend   land
5. guess   gas

Dictation Practice

Write the next five words recorded on the CD on a piece of paper. When you finish, check your answers with the list below.

Spelling Challenge

Now write the next three sentences you hear recorded on the CD.

Check your work below.

Answers to Exercises

Recognition Practice, p. 37 pass, here, we're, land, ear

Dictation Practice, p. 37 we're, mean, steer, laugh, man

Recognition Practice, p. 38 men, pan, ran, lend, gas

Dictation Practice, laughed, guess, man, messed, pen

Spelling Challenge, There were three people here. Where were you? I can can the tomatoes.

Unit Twelve
The Sound /eiy/

Introducing the Sound

This is a combination of sounds. Begin with your lips in the first position of /eə/, about ½ inch (1.3 cm) apart and with a wide, downward smile. Then, slowly widen them into an upward smile, forming /iy/. (See Figure 12.)

The tongue is low, then raises to mid position. Count to two silently to be sure the sound is long enough.

Figure 12.
The sound /eiy/

Listen to the examples and repeat them after the speaker.

EXAMPLES

a_e	*ay*	*e*	*au*	*ai*	*aigh*	*ey*
ate face	day way	café	gauge	pain	straight	prey they
ace base came fate haze mane pale race wave	bay fray gray hay jay lay may pay pray say	suede		fail faint gain main pail quail rain sail tail vain waiver		grey hey Seychelles

et	ée	eig	ei	ea
ballet	fiancée	**eig**ht	rein	gr**ea**t
buff**et**	brûl**ée**	d**eig**n **feig**n	f**ei**nt h**ei**nous	

Move your lips into the /ə/ position after /**eiy**/ when it occurs before the consonant /l/. Listen to the examples and repeat them after the speaker.

EXAMPLES

p**a**le	s**ai**l	th**ey**'ll

Practice for Mastery

Repeat the following sentences which feature the sound /**eiy**/.

EXAMPLES

It rained **eig**ht d**ay**s.
The su**e**de cape has *a* gr**ea**t shape.
R**e**n**ee** **a**te creme brul**ee** at th**e** buff**et** today.
Th**e** r**ai**n in Sp**ai**n st**ay**s m**ai**nly in th**e** pl**ai**n.
She l**ai**d th**e** fr**ai**l l**a**ce on th**e** table.

Contrasting Sound Practice

To compare the sound /ɛ/, from Unit Eight, with /**eiy**/, repeat the following words.

EXAMPLES

/ɛ/	/eiy/	/ɛ/	/eiy/
red	raid	pen	pane, pain
bet	bait	wren	rain, rein, reign
debt	date	test	taste
fell	fail	shed	shade
get	gate	tent	taint
mess	mace		

Now repeat several sentences that feature both sounds.

Fred's cake failed the taste test.
Get the red dress for your date.
Jane's friend fell on the train.
Sell ten shares and trade the rest.

Recognition Practice

Five words with the sounds /ɛ/ and /**eiy**/ are recorded next. Circle below the words you hear, then check them below.

Exercise

1. pen   pain
2. test   taste
3. debt   date
4. fell   fail
5. get   gate

Dictation Practice

Five words containing these sounds are recorded next on the CD. Write them during the pauses, then check them below.

Spelling Challenge

Seven sentences containing words with confusing spelling are recorded next. Listen and write them down during the pauses. Check them below.

Answers to Exercises

Recognition Practice, pain, test, debt, fail, get

Dictation Practice, red, bait, shade, fell, mess

Spelling Challenge, The pain came again. Her friend is a fiend for french fries. There were many zany women. The ape ate eight apples and an apricot. Hey, where's the key? She said she was afraid. The players said their prayers and paid their debts.

Unit Thirteen
The Sound /ɔ/

Introducing the Sound

To make the vowel sound /ɔ/, drop your jaw until the lips are ⅝ inch (1.5 cm) apart. Tense your lips and round them forward halfway. (See Figure 13.)

The tongue is in low position.

The sound is long.

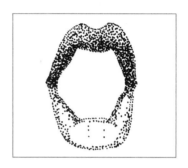

Figure 13.
The sound /ɔ/

Listen to the examples and repeat them after the speaker.

Examples

o	a	au	augh	aw	ou	ough	oa
off on often gone	all call	auto fault	daughter caught	awful lawn	cough	bought	broad
boss coffee cost cross foster lost toss	ball fall gall hall mall tall wall	gaunt haul haunt maul Paul	naught taught	bawdy bawl crawl jaw law raw saw tawdry		brought fought ought sought thought wrought	

Practice for Mastery

Listen to the following sentences featuring the sound /ɔ/, and repeat them after the speaker.

EXAMPLES

> Draw water from the faucet.
> The water *is* always calm in August.
> I thought Audrey saw *a* lawyer.
> You ought to have brought your daughter.

Contrasting Sound Practice

To compare /ʌ/, from Unit Seven, with /ɔ/, repeat these words after the speaker.

EXAMPLES

/ʌ/	/ɔ/	/ʌ/	/ɔ/
cuff	cough	sung	song
gun	gone	rung	wrong
but	bought	cut	caught
lung	long	gulf	golf

Now, say the next sentences after the speaker.

EXAMPLES

> Bud was caught with the gun he bought.
> Sunny has sung all the wrong love songs.
> Audrey bought the awesome puppies.
> Maud cut the cuffs from that awful cloth.

Recognition Practice

Listen to the next five words recorded on the CD, and circle below the ones you hear. The answers are on page 45.

EXERCISE

1. lung   long
2. cut   caught
3. gun   gone
4. cut   caught
5. gulf   golf

Dictation Practice

Now write the next five words recorded on the CD on a piece of paper, then check your answers on page 45.

Contrasting Sound Practice

To compare /**ow**/, from Unit Nine, with /ɔ/, repeat the following words.

EXAMPLES

/ow/	/ɔ/	/ow/	/ɔ/
loan	lawn	loafed	loft
boat	bought	bowl	ball
coat	caught	own	on
oaf	off	boast	bossed

Now say these sentences after the speaker.

EXAMPLES

Joe caught the mole in his lawn.
Paula lost her coat on the long walk.
The tall author is his own boss.
He bought the old boat, then walked home.

Recognition Practice

Listen to the next five words recorded on the CD, and circle the ones you hear. Check your answers below.

EXERCISE

1. loafed	loft
2. coat	caught
3. bowl	ball
4. boast	bossed
5. loan	lawn

Dictation Practice

Now write the five words recorded next on the CD on a piece of paper. Check your answers below.

Spelling Challenge

Write the four sentences recorded on the tape during the pauses, then check them below.

Answers to Exercises

Recognition Practice, p. 44 lung, cut, gone, caught, golf

Dictation Practice, p. 44 song, but, gulf, cough, cuff

Recognition Practice, loafed, caught, bowl, boast, lawn

Dictation Practice, off, own, coat, bought, loaf

Spelling Challenge, The wolf plays golf. He laughed when he was caught with the faux diamond. Although the rough cough went through him, he was tough. She has gone and done it alone.

Unit Fourteen
The Sound /æ/

Introducing the Sound

To make this sound, keep your lips ⅝ inch (1.5 cm) apart and form a half-smile, with tense lips. (See Figure 14.)

The tongue is in low position.

The sound is short.

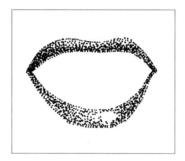

Figure 14.
The sound /æ/

Listen to the examples and repeat them after the speaker.

EXAMPLES

a	*ai*	*e*
back	plaid	meringue
cat		
tap		
bag		
pad		
cab		
action		
black		
crab		
fabulous		
gash		
had		
jack		

a	*ai*	*e*
knack		
lack		
master		
naturally		
sash		

Practice for Mastery

Listen to the following sentences featuring the sound /æ/, and repeat them after the speaker.

EXAMPLES

> Pack the bags.
> Have *a* snack, Jack.
> Pat's cat is fat.
> Her plaid jacket has black snaps.

Contrasting Sound Practice

To compare /iy/, from Unit Four, with /æ/, repeat the following words after the speaker.

EXAMPLES

/iy/	/æ/	/iy/	/æ/
feet, feat	fat	heed, he'd	had
seat	sat	he's	has
seed	sad	heat	hat
leap	lap	neat	gnat

Now repeat these sentences.

EXAMPLES

> Please feed the cats.
> He needs *a* black hat.
> Matt has *a* shack near the sea.
> She believes that Pete has had *a* nap.

Recognition Practice

Five words featuring these sounds are recorded next on the CD. Below, circle the ones you hear, then check the answers on page 49.

EXERCISE

1. feet   fat
2. leap   lap
3. he'd   had
4. seed   sad
5. heat   hat

Dictation Practice

Write the next five words recorded on the CD on a piece of paper. When you finish, check your work on page 49.

Contrasting Sound Practice

Compare the /ɛ/ of Unit Eight with /æ/ by repeating each word after the speaker.

EXAMPLES

/ɛ/	/æ/	/ɛ/	/æ/
beg	bag	wreck	rack
head	had	set	sat
met	mat	said	sad
pet	pat	pled	plaid

Listen to the following sentences that feature /ɛ/ and /æ/, and repeat them after the speaker.

The pet cat sat on the bed.
Pat had a red rag on her head.
The men said it had a sad ending.
The next guest patted Fred on the back.

Recognition Practice

Five words featuring these sounds are recorded next on the CD. Circle them below, then check them further below.

EXERCISE

1. met	mat
2. set	sat
3. wreck	rack
4. head	had
5. said	sad

Dictation Practice

Write the next five words recorded on the CD on a piece of paper. When you finish, check your words below.

Answers to Exercises

Recognition Practice, p. 48 fat, leap, he'd, sad, heat

Dictation Practice, p. 48 sad, has, he's, seed, feet or feat

Recognition Practice, mat, set, wreck, had, sad

Dictation Practice, head, pet, said, rack, beg

Unit Fifteen
The Sound /æow/

Introducing the Sound

This is a combination of vowel sounds. Begin with /**æ**/ by setting your lips ⅝ inch (1.5 cm) apart; then, glide into /**ow**/, forming a circle with your lips. (See Figure 15.)

The tongue is in low position.

The sound is long.

Figure 15.
The sound /æow/

Listen to the examples and repeat them after the speaker.

EXAMPLES

ow	ou	ough
how now brown	house aloud	**bough**
allow brow cow down frown gown jowls vow vowel	bout clout devout doubt gout lousy mouse pout rout snout	

To pronounce /æow/ before the consonant /r/, begin with /æow/, move your lips to the /ə/ position, then round them and push them outward into the /r/ position. This is a very long vowel sound.

Repeat the examples of the sound /æowər/.

EXAMPLES

our	*auer*	*ower*
sour flour hour	sauerkraut	power
devour dour		bower cower shower

Practice for Mastery

Now, repeat the following sentences featuring the sound /æow/.

EXAMPLES

> **Ou**r townh**ou**se has *a* br**ow**n m**ou**se.
> Are we all**ow**ed t**o** speak al**ou**d?
> We f**ou**nd **ou**r g**ow**ns d**ow**nt**ow**n.
> Sh**ow**er the fl**ow**ers f**o**r *a*n h**ou**r.
> H**ow**'s the sau**e**rkr**au**t?

Spelling Challenge

The next nine sentences, which contain words with tricky spelling, are recorded on the CD. Write them during the pauses, then check your work below.

Answers to Exercise

Spelling Challenge, Ouch! Don't touch me. You found out you could wound him. She wound the bandage around the wound. Slow down now. It's snowing. The rouge covered the gouge. It's my own gown. Of course the mouse couldn't eat the mousse, but my cousin could. He's the flower grower. On a tour of the mill, we bought four bags of flour.

UNIT SIXTEEN
THE SOUND /a/

Introducing the Sound

To make this sound, drop your jaw until the lips are about ¾ inch (2 cm) apart, but relaxed. (See Figure 16.)

The tongue is in low position.

The sound is short but takes a little longer because your mouth is open so wide!

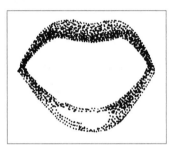

Figure 16.
The sound /a/

Listen to the examples and repeat them after the speaker.

EXAMPLES

a	*o*	*ho*	*e*	*ow*	*eau*
father wand	cot doll lock **o**ption	**ho**nor **ho**nest	encore ennui	knowledge	bureaucracy
wad waffle wander	bomb doctor fond gosh hot lot motley not pond rot sob toddler		genre		

Practice for Mastery

Listen to the following sentences featuring the sound /**a**/, and repeat them after the speaker.

EXAMPLES

Roz *is* fond of dolls.
John got *an* honest job.
Bob stopped in the shop for *a* mop.
His knowledge of crops *is* obvious.

Contrasting Sound Practice

Compare /ʌ/, from Unit Seven, with /**a**/. Repeat these words after the speaker.

EXAMPLES

/ʌ/	/**a**/	/ʌ/	/**a**/
hut	hot	shut	shot
buddy	body	putt	pot
cup	cop	gut	got
rut	rot	nut	not, knot

Now say the following sentences.

EXAMPLES

Her brother got *a* hot supper.
Some shots *are* optional.
Buddy dropped the hot cup in the shop.
Stop fussing *and* come up.

Recognition Practice

Five words featuring these sounds are recorded next on the CD. Circle the ones you hear, then check them on page 55.

1. buddy	body
2. hut	hot
3. shut	shot
4. hut	hot
5. nut	not

Dictation Practice

Listen to the next five words on the CD and write them on a piece of paper during the pauses. Check them on page 55 when you finish.

The /**a**/ when followed by /**r**/, ends with the lips pushed outward; this changes the sound somewhat.

Listen to the examples and repeat them after the speaker, then listen for the confirmation.

Examples

arm	b*a*zaar	gu*a*rd	serge*a*nt
ark			
far			heart
carve			

Practice for Mastery

Listen to the following sentences, which contain the /**a**/ sound followed by /**r**/, and repeat them after the speaker.

Examples

Are the stars far from Mars?
The hard part is to start the car.
Sergeant Barton was the guard.
He carved a large heart in the bark.

Spelling Challenge

During the pauses, write the next six sentences you hear on the CD. Check your work below.

Answers to Exercises

Recognition Practice, p. 54 body, hut, shut, hot, nut

Dictation Practice, p. 54 cop, shot, buddy, cup, knot or not

Spelling Challenge, We're here to honor the donor. Don't bother my brother or my father. They found a comb and a bomb in the tomb. Ron's son won the ribbon. Please polish the Polish medal. It's warm on the farm.

CD 2
TRACK
1

UNIT SEVENTEEN
THE SOUND /aiy/

Introducing the Sound

The /**aiy**/ sound is a double vowel. Begin sounding the /**a**/, with the lips about ¾ inch (2 cm) apart. Then move your lips to the /**iy**/ position, forming a big smile. (See Figure 17.)

The tongue is in low position.

This is a long sound.

Figure 17.
The sound /aiy/

Listen to the examples, repeat them after the speaker, then listen for the confirmation.

EXAMPLES

i	*ie*	*igh*	*oi*	*ai*	*ei*
I **I**'d **i**ce b**i**ke	p**ie** dr**ie**d	m**igh**t	ch**oi**r	**ai**sle	h**ei**ght
bilin**gu**al d**ie**t d**i**ssect h**i**de **i**ce k**i**te p**i**ke qu**ie**t	cr**ie**d d**ie** v**ie**	f**igh**t fl**igh**t h**igh** l**igh**t m**igh**t n**igh**t pl**igh**t r**igh**t			

i	*ie*	*igh*	*oi*	*ai*	*ei*
quite rice side tire wide		sigh sight tight			

ia	*y*	*ui*	*uy*	*ye*	*ic*	*ig*
diaper	my fly	guide	guy buy	rye	indict	
	sky why			eye		sign malign design

Practice for Mastery

Listen to the following sentences featuring the sound /**aiy**/, and repeat them after the speaker.

EXAMPLES

Ida buys nice surprises.
I'm twice your size, Liza!
Try my pie, Ira!
That guy might buy my cycle.

Spelling Challenge

During the pauses, write the next three sentences you hear on the CD, then check your work below.

Answers to Exercise

Spelling Challenge, Write down your height and weight. The police officers are nice and polite. I find that the wind bothers my brother.

PART TWO
English Consonant Sounds

Consonant sounds are determined by

- the position of the tongue, lips, and teeth
- the way air is released
- the use of, or absence of, voice

Study Figure 18, then follow the directions for each sound.

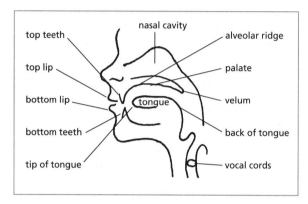

Figure 18.

Unit Eighteen
The Sounds /p/, /b/

Introducing the Sound /p/

To make the sound /**p**/, put your lips together firmly, stop the air completely, then pop the lips open. Do not make a vocal sound. (See Figure 19.)

At the beginning of words, release /**p**/ with a puff of air. To be sure the puff of air is strong enough, place a small piece of paper in front of your mouth when pronouncing the following words. The paper should move considerably.

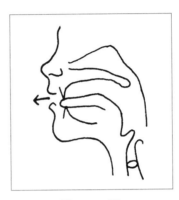

Figure 19.
The sound /p/

Listen to the following examples and repeat them after the speaker.

Examples

pay	**p**it	**p**lay
pat	**p**ot	**p**raise
peck		

Make the same puff of air when a word ends in another consonant plus /**p**/.

Listen to the following examples and repeat them after the speaker.

lam**p**	har**p**	gras**p**	scal**p**
lim**p**	shar**p**	was**p**	hel**p**

Do not make the puff of air when /**p**/ occurs in the middle of a word before a vowel sound.

Listen to the following examples and repeat them after the speaker.

a**pp**le (pəl)	sim**p**le (pəl)	pur**p**le (pəl)
ha**pp**y	peo**p**le (pəl)	

Do not make the puff of air when /**p**/ directly follows the sound /**s**/ at the beginning or in the middle of a word.

Listen to the examples and repeat them after the speaker.

s**p**an	whis**p**er
s**p**end	hos**p**it*a*l
s**p**ill	as**p**i*r*i*n*
s**p**oil	e**xp**ect

When /**p**/ is the last sound in a word and is followed by another word, do not pop your lips open. Bring the lips together firmly, making no vocal sound, then say the next word.

Listen to the following sentences and repeat them after the speaker.

Put the top down.
Keep trying.
I hope to stop them.
It's up there.
The map you gave me is helpful.

When /p/ is the last sound, make it either with or without the puff of air. There is no difference in meaning.

Listen to the following examples of sentences read both ways and repeat them after the speaker.

With the puff	Without the puff
Stop!	Stop!
Read the map.	Read the map.
Let's go on *a* trip.	Let's go on *a* trip.
I need some sleep.	I need some sleep.
Never give up.	Never give up.

Practice for Mastery

Listen to the following sentences featuring the sound /p/, and repeat them after the speaker.

Please prepare the pizza for the party.
Pat helped me pick up the papers.
Put the stamps on the package.
Mr. Bishop paid for the lamp in April.
Phillip didn't give me *a* map.
Penny has the hiccoughs.

About the Letter p

The letter p followed by the letter h is usually pronounced /f/.

The letter p is silent (not pronounced) in the following words. Listen, and repeat each word after the speaker.

EXAMPLES

receipt	corps	cupboard
psychology	raspberry	sapphire
pneumonia		

Introducing the Sound /b/

To pronounce /b/, place your lips together firmly; stop the air completely, and make a voiced sound. (See Figure 20.)

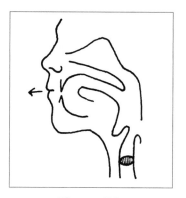

Figure 20.
The sound /b/

Listen to the following examples and repeat them after the speaker.

EXAMPLES

bag	ru**bb**er
bread	so**bb**ed
bul**b**	
o**bs**erve	
ca**b**s	

Practice for Mastery

Listen to the following sentences featuring the sound /**b**/, and repeat them after the speaker.

EXAMPLES

Billy gra**bb**ed the so**bb**ing **b**a**b**y.
The **b**ushes and **b**ul**b**s are a**b**out to **b**loom.
Bo**b** was **b**leeding, and his **b**ones were **b**roken.
May**b**e Eliza**b**eth **b**rags a **b**it.

About the Letter <u>b</u>

The letter <u>b</u> is silent in the following words. Listen, and repeat each word after the speaker.

EXAMPLES

debt	comb	subtle
doubt	tomb	subpoena
lamb	womb	

Contrasting Sound Practice

Compare the sound /**p**/ with the sound /**b**/ by repeating the following words after the speaker.

EXAMPLES

/p/	/b/
pin	**b**in
pet	**b**et
pack	**b**ack
pole	**b**owl
push	**b**ush
pour, **p**ore	**b**ore, **b**oar
punch	**b**unch
prayed	**b**raid
re**p**el	re**b**el
ra**p**id	ra**b**id
ro**p**ed	ro**b**ed
ri**pp**ed	ri**bb**ed
pare, **p**air, **p**ear	**b**are, **b**ear

Recognition Practice

Listen to the next four sentences recorded on the CD. Circle the ones you hear, or repeat the sentences now and do the written exercise later. The correct answers are below.

EXERCISE

1. I can't pare it.   I can't bear it.
2. Paul needs a push in   Paul needs a bush in
   front of his house.   front of his house.
3. We bought a big pole.   We bought a big bowl.
4. Patty has some new cups.   Patty has some new cubs.

Answers to Exercise

Recognition Practice, I can't bear it. Paul needs a push in front of his house. We bought a big pole. Patty has some new cubs.

Unit Nineteen
The Sounds /t/, /d/

Introducing the Sound /t/

Place the tip of the tongue against the alveolar ridge, stop the air completely, then release the air. (See Figure 21.) Do not make a vocal sound.

There are several variations of this consonant.

Figure 21.
The sound /t/

When a word begins with /t/, make the sound with a noisy puff of air.

To be sure the puff of air is noisy enough, hold a small piece of paper in front of your mouth when pronouncing the following words. It should move considerably.

Listen to the following examples and repeat them after the speaker.

Examples

tame	ten	tray	**th**yme
tap	tip	tree	
team		twin	
		twelve	

Make the same noisy puff when a word ends in another consonant sound plus /t/.

67

Listen to the examples and repeat them after the speaker.

act	apt
lift	last
fault	borscht
can't	text

Usage Tips

- Make the same noisy puff for **-st** or **-est** at the end of an adjective to make the superlative form.

Listen to the examples and repeat them after the speaker.

best	worst	most
biggest	smallest	least
happiest	silliest	

- The past tense marker, <u>ed</u>, is pronounced /t/, with the puff of air, when the verb ends in a voiceless consonant sound such as /**p**/, /**k**/, /**ch**/, /**f**/, /**sh**/, /**s**/, or /**ks**/. Be careful not to make a vowel sound before the /**t**/.

Listen to the examples and repeat them after the speaker.

taped	washed
picked	passed
watched	faxed
laughed	

Do not make the puff of air when /**t**/ follows /**s**/ at the beginning of a syllable.

EXAMPLES

stamp	mistake
step	faster
stove	history

- To pronounce /t/ just before the sound /s/ at the end of words, tap the tip of your tongue on the palate, then slide your tongue forward to make /s/.

Listen to the examples and repeat them after the speaker.

EXAMPLES

bats	cats
rests	beasts
bites	coats

To produce the /t/ at the end of words that occur before words beginning with a consonant, tap your tongue on the alveolar ridge, stop the vocal sound, then go on to the next word.

Listen to the examples and repeat them after the speaker.

EXAMPLES

She ate three hot dogs.
The fat cat sat down on the mat.
I'll bet she got the hat with that money.
I met them at the market.

In certain words, the /t/ is unreleased as above, then followed by the unstressed vowel sound /ə/, then by the sound /n/.

Listen to the examples and repeat them after the speaker.

EXAMPLES

button	fountain	important
mitten	mountain	sentence
kitten		
bitten		

When the last word you say ends in the sound /t/, pronounce it either with or without the puff of air. There is no difference in meaning.

Listen to the following sentences read both ways, and repeat them after the speaker.

EXAMPLES

With the puff	Without the puff
He sat on his hat.	He sat on his hat.
She put on her coat.	She put on her coat.
They came to visit.	They came to visit.
He didn't eat.	He didn't eat.
I didn't say that.	I didn't say that.

Practice for Mastery

Listen to the following sentences featuring the sound /t/, and repeat them after the speaker.

EXAMPLES

Those tenants tore up the apartment.
Leave the stew on the stove for two minutes.
Just a minute, please.
I put the buttons in my pocket.
Stand up straight.
Janet washed her skirt and two t-shirts.
She wished she had polished her boots.
The last time I went to that store, I got lost.

About the Letter t

The letter t, when followed by the sound /iuw/ is usually pronounced /ch/. (See Unit Twenty-two, page 91.)

When the letter t occurs between vowels, it has one of the pronunciations of the sound /d/. (See Introducing the Sound /d/, which follows.)

The letter t is silent in the following words. Listen, and repeat each word after the speaker.

EXAMPLES

often	fasten	mortgage
listen	hasten	mustn't

See Unit Twenty-nine for the pronunciation of the letter t followed by h.

Introducing the Sound /d/

To make the sound /d/ place the tip of the tongue on the alveolar ridge and make a voiced sound. (See Figure 22.)

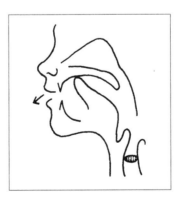

Figure 22.
The sound /d/

Hold the /d/ slightly at the beginning of a word, then release it with the next sound.

Listen to the examples and repeat them after the speaker.

day	**d**ress	**d**warf
dime	**d**rive	
does		
doll*a*r		
do		

At the end of words, before consonants, hold your tongue briefly on the alveolar ridge, then go on to the next word.

Listen to the examples and repeat them after the speaker.

Tell da**d** t*o* drive.
Th*e* be**d** b*e*longs t*o* me.
Th*e* li**d** fell off.
When d*oe*s th*e* ti**d**e come in?
Th*e* co**d**e numb*e*r *i*s on th*e* back.

To make the sound of /**d**/ between vowels and after the consonant /**r**/, tap the tongue quickly on the palate without holding it, then go on to the next vowel.

Note that this sound is often spelled with the letters <u>*dd*</u>, <u>t</u>, and <u>tt</u>.

Listen to the examples and repeat them after the speaker.

la**d**y	mu**dd**y	grat*e*d
bo**d**y	**a**dde**d**	subt*le* (əl)
fa**d**ed	city	
gra**d**ed	later	litt*le*
har**d**er	shorter	fitte**d**
or**d**er		
da**dd**y		

Usage Tips

- To make the regular past tense, add /**d**/ to verbs that end in a vowel sound or one of the voiced consonants /**b**/, /**g**/, /**v**/, /**j**/, /**l**/, /**m**/, /**n**/, /**r**/, /**z**/, /**w**/, or /**y**/. Even though there is a letter e before the letter d, do not make a vowel sound before the /**d**/. The e is silent.

Listen to the examples and repeat them after the speaker.

EXAMPLES

playe**d**	rubbe**d**	hemme**d**
staye**d**	hugge**d**	canne**d**
crie**d**	love**d**	feare**d**
snowe**d**	judge**d**	buzze**d**
glue**d**	rolle**d**	

- Add the unstressed vowel /ə/ plus /**d**/ to verbs ending with the sound /**d**/ or /**t**/. The verb now has one more syllable.

Listen to the examples and repeat them after the speaker.

EXAMPLES

fade**d**	wante**d**
ende**d**	plante**d**
lande**d**	invite**d**
folde**d**	create**d**
loade**d**	greete**d**

- A pronoun plus '/**d**/ forms a contraction for the modals had and would. Be careful to not use the unstressed vowel /ə/ here, which would add another syllable to the word.

Listen to the examples and repeat them after the speaker.

I'**d** been there before.	(I had been there before.)
They'**d** called us earlier.	(They had called us earlier.)
We'**d** better stay.	(We had better stay.)
You'**d** better not do that.	(You had better not do that.)
I'**d** help you *if* I could.	(I would help you if I could.)
He'**d** come *if* he wanted to.	(He would come if he wanted to.)
We'**d** like *a* drink.	(We would like a drink.)

Practice for Mastery

Listen to the following sentences featuring the sound /**d**/, and repeat them after the speaker.

Dan **d**rove us *a*round before **d**inner.
Does **D**onn*a* have *a* **d**oll*a*r?
David **d**i**d**n't **d**o the **d**ishes.

He sai**d** it.
I got it.
She di**d** it.

That be**d** is ol**d**.
She ha**d** *a* ba**d** col**d**.
He ate *a* bit of butter.

Fred *is a* forty-year-ol**d** veter*a*n.
Patty sat on the little la**dd**er.
Eddy's thirty to**d**ay.
It's *a* beaut*if*ul city, b*u*t it's so dirty!

About the Letter <u>d</u>

The letter <u>d</u> followed by the sound /**iuw**/ is usually pronounced /**j**/. (See Unit Twenty-two, page 92.)

The letter <u>d</u> is silent in the following words. Listen, and repeat each word after the speaker.

EXAMPLES

> Wednesday
> grandfather
> grandmother
> grandchildren
> handkerchief

Practice in Context

Listen to the following poem featuring the final past tense sounds /**t**/, /**d**/, and /**əd**/, and repeat each line after the speaker.

The Surprise Party

/**t**/
They shopped, spent, cooked, ate,
Drank, gossiped, laughed, baked,
Stopped *a*nd talked,
Worked *a*nd walked.
/**d**/
They planned, saved, sewed, schemed,
Programmed, whispered, giggled, dreamed,
Enjoyed and played,
A party made.
/**əd**/
They decorat*e*d *a*nd wait*e*d,
Then shout*e*d *a*nd celebrat*e*d.

Now listen to a tongue twister that features the sounds /t/ and /d/, and repeat each line after the speaker.

The Tutor

A tutor who tooted the flute
Tried to teach two young tooters to toot,
Said the two to the tutor:
"Is it harder to toot,
or to tutor two tooters to toot?"

Unit Twenty
The Sounds /k/, /g/

Introducing the Sound /k/

To pronounce /**k**/, bring the back of the tongue to the velum, stop the air completely, then release it with a voiceless sound. (See Figure 23.)

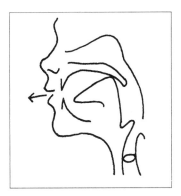

Figure 23.
The sound /k/

At the beginning of words, release /**k**/ with a puff of air. To make sure the puff of air is strong enough, hold a small piece of paper in front of your mouth as you say the following words. The paper should move considerably.

Listen to the following examples, and repeat them after the speaker.

EXAMPLES

cat	**c**lean	**k**ettl*e* (əl)
cost	**c**razy	
		khaki

Make the same puff of air when a word ends in another consonant plus /**k**/.

Listen to the following examples, and repeat them after the speaker.

fran**k**	wor**k**	as**k**	tal**k**
in**k**	for**k**		wal**k**
		mos**q**ue	

Do not make the puff of air when /**k**/ is followed by the sound /**w**/.

Listen to the examples and repeat them after the speaker.

quick
queen
question
quite

Do not make the puff when /**k**/ occurs in the middle of a word before a vowel sound.

Listen to the following examples, and repeat them after the speaker.

lan**k**y	sti**ck**y	un**cl**e (əl)	la**cqu**er
as**k**ing	ti**ck**le (əl)	cho**c**olate	
mon**k**ey	wi**ck**ed		sa**cch**arine

When /**k**/ occurs just after the sound /**s**/, there is no puff of air.

Listen to the following examples, and repeat them after the speaker.

EXAMPLES

skin	school
skate	schedule
basket	
scrape	

When /k/ occurs just before another consonant, bring the back of the tongue to the velum, stop the air briefly, but do not release it; then make the next sound.

Listen to the examples, and repeat them after the speaker.

EXAMPLES

asks	asked	action (ak shən)
likes	liked	actor
bakes	baked	picture (pik chər)
		anxious (aŋk shəs)

Listen to the following sentences, and repeat them after the speaker.

EXAMPLES

Pick the music up tomorrow.
Look at the black bike over there.
I'll make a cake in the morning.
Did Rick rake the leaves?
Luke fell off his bike and scraped his skin.

When /k/ is the last sound in a word or sentence, pronounce it with or without the puff of air. There is no difference in meaning.

Listen to the following examples of sentences read both ways and repeat them after the speaker.

EXAMPLES

With the puff	Without the puff
Don't loo**k**!	Don't loo**k**!
That's *a* fa**k**e.	That's *a* fa**k**e.
I have *a* stom*a***ch** a**ch**e.	I have *a* stom*a***ch** a**ch**e.

Practice for Mastery

Listen to the following sentences featuring the sound /**k**/, and repeat them after the speaker.

EXAMPLES

Can you **c**ut the **c**ake for me?
Carolyn couldn't **c**ome to the **c**oncert.
His wi**ck**ed un**c**le has no s**c**ruples.
Mi**k**e and Ja**ck** **c**an wor**k** **q**ui**ck**ly.
He wal**k**s to the ban**k** every day.
They tal**k**ed and as**k**ed **q**uestions.

About the Letters k and c

The letter **k** is not pronounced in the following words. Listen, and repeat each word after the speaker.

EXAMPLES

know	knowledge	knife
knew	knee	blackguard

The letter **c** is silent in the following word. Listen, and repeat after the speaker.

EXAMPLES

indict

Introducing the Sound /g/

CD 2
TRACK
6

To make the sound /**g**/, bring the back of the tongue to the velum, stop the air briefly, then release it with a voiced sound. (See Figure 24.)

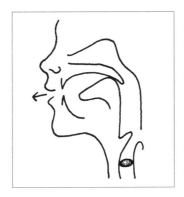

Figure 24.
The sound /g/

Listen and repeat the examples after the speaker.

EXAMPLES

game	e**gg**	**gh**ost
glad	e**gg**s	
grade	bi**gg**er	
	ru**gg**ed	

Practice for Mastery

Listen to the following sentences featuring the sound /**g**/, and repeat them after the speaker.

EXAMPLES

Go **g**et y**ou**r **g**randmother's **g**las**s**es.
Pe**gg**y be**gg**ed t**o g**o to the art **g**all**e**ry.
Glori**a g**ives **g**raci**ou**s **g**et-to**g**eth**e**rs.
Please **g**ive me eight **g**all**o**ns **o**f **g**as.
Ma**gg**ie ba**gg**ed all th**e g**roc**e**ries.
Gayle dra**gg**ed th**e** ru**gg**ed lu**gg**a**g**e through th**e g**ate.

Contrasting Sound Practice

To compare /**g**/ with /**k**/, repeat the following words after the speaker.

EXAMPLES

/k/	/g/	/k/	/g/
cot	got	back	bag
cane	gain	pick	pig
came	game	hawk	hog
come	gum	bicker	bigger
clean	glean	sacked	sagged
curl	girl	tacked, tact	tagged
rack	rag		

Recognition Practice

The speaker will read four sentences. Circle the ones you hear, or repeat them during the pauses and do the written exercise later. The answers are on page 83.

EXERCISE

1. Gary got a clean rag.   Gary got a clean rack.
2. He is just like a hawk.   He is just like a hog.
3. We need the glue.   We need the clue.
4. Please put it in the back.   Please put it in the bag.

About the Letter g

The letter g after the letter <u>n</u> has the sound /ŋ/. See Unit Twenty-six, page 116.

The letter g is not pronounced in the following words. Listen, and repeat each word after the speaker.

EXAMPLES

phlegm	caught, taught	weight, eight
di*a*phragm	bought, brought	might, light
sign	through	campaign
champagne	though	reign
lasagn*a*	height	

Answers to Exercise

Recognition Practice, p. 82 Gary got a clean rag. He is just like a hawk. We need the glue. Please put it in the back.

UNIT TWENTY-ONE
THE SOUNDS /f/, /v/

Introducing the Sound /f/

To make the sound /**f**/, place the top teeth firmly on the inside of the bottom lip; release the air continuously with no voice. (See Figure 25.)

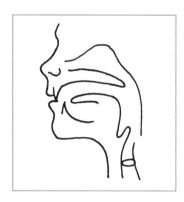

Figure 25.
The sound /f/

Listen to the examples and repeat them after the speaker.

EXAMPLES

fall	ha**lf**	sa**pph**ire
fish		
food	o**ft**en	lau**gh**
fresh		lau**gh**s
flower	**ph**one	lau**gh**ed
a**ft**er	tro**ph**y	tou**gh**
	Ral**ph**	cou**gh**
ba**ff**le(əl)	Ral**ph**'s	
pu**ff**ed		
mu**ff**		

Practice for Mastery

Listen to the following sentences and repeat them after the speaker.

EXAMPLES

Freddy found fresh flowers for his friend.
Francie lifted her finger to show off her sapphire.
Ralph's life is tough, but he laughs.
Phil's life is soft, but he frets.
He ate the fish and half a loaf of bread, then left.

Contrasting Sound Practice

Compare the sound /p/, from Unit Eighteen with /f/ by repeating the following words after the speaker.

EXAMPLES

/p/	/f/	/p/	/f/
pin	fin	pile	file
peel	feel	pour	four
pine	fine	pray	fray
paid	fade	pride	fried
pail	fail	pieced	feast
pare, pair, pear	fare, fair	pup	puff
peer	fear	sipped	sift
pork	fork	ripped	rift

Recognition Practice

The speaker will read four sentences on the CD. Circle the ones you hear, or repeat them now and do the written exercise later. The answers are on page 89.

Exercise

1. Please peel this fruit.   Please feel this fruit.
2. It's a pine floor.   It's a fine floor.
3. She needs the pork   She needs the fork
   to make the pie.   to make the pie.
4. How much is the pair?   How much is the fair?

Practice in Context

Now, after the speaker, repeat each line of the following poem featuring the /**p**/ and /**f**/ sounds.

One fresh fall day
Paul went to the fair
To find some fun and food.
But while hopping a fence
He ripped his pants,
Which put him in a foul mood.
But he found a fine friend
And prayed she would mend
The rip before it could fray;
And although he was pieced
With a patch on the seat
He went to the feast anyway.

Introducing the Sound /v/

To make the sound /v/, place the upper teeth against the inside of the lower lip, and release the air with a voiced sound. (See Figure 26.)

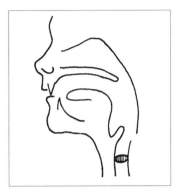

Figure 26.
The sound /v/

Listen to the following examples, repeat them after the speaker, then listen for the confirmation.

EXAMPLES

vine	save	saves
vote	five	believes
favor	believe	saved
ever		loved
envy	of	

Usage Tip

* The contractions of <u>I have</u>, <u>you have</u>, <u>we have</u>, and <u>they have</u> are formed by adding an apostrophe ('ve) to the pronoun.

Listen to the examples and repeat them after the speaker.

I've been there.	(I have been there.)
You've seen it.	(You have seen it.)
We've won.	(We have won.)
They've gone.	(They have gone.)

Practice for Mastery

Listen to the following sentences and repeat them after the speaker.

Evelyn arrived in evening gloves at eleven.
Val survived the five-hour drive.
She is obviously envious, and I love it.
It takes a lot of nerve to drive over there in the van.
They've never voted in Virginia before.

Contrasting Sound Practice

Compare the sound /b/, from Unit Eighteen with /v/. Listen to the following words, and repeat them after the speaker.

/b/	/v/	/b/	/v/
bet	vet	ballet	valet
base	vase	bent	vent
berry, bury	very	best	vest
buys	vise	marble	marvel
bail, bale	veil, vale	Serbs	serves

Recognition Practice

Four sentences are recorded on the CD. Circle the ones you hear, or repeat them during the pauses and do the written exercise later. The answers are below.

When you have mastered these, try recording them on tape to compare your pronunciation with that of the speaker.

EXERCISE

1. She's a good bet.	She's a good vet.
2. We want to see the ballet.	We want to see the valet.
3. I only want the best.	I only want the vest.
4. Bev's bail was stiff.	Bev's veil was stiff.

Answers to Exercises

Recognition Practice, p. 86 Please feel this fruit. It's a pine floor. She needs the fork to make the pie. How much is the pair?

Recognition Practice, She's a good vet. We want to see the ballet. I only want the best. Bev's veil was stiff.

UNIT TWENTY-TWO
THE SOUNDS /ch/, /j/

Introducing the Sound /ch/

To make the sound /**ch**/, place the center of the tongue on the palate; stop the air completely, then release it abruptly with a voiceless sound. (See Figure 27.)

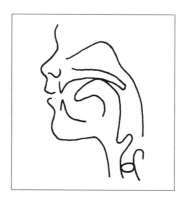

Figure 27.
The sound /ch/

Listen to the examples and repeat them after the speaker.

EXAMPLES

chase	ca**tch**	ques**ti**on
chance	ca**tch**ing	
rea**ch**ing	ca**tch**es	
lun**ch**	wa**tch**ed	
lun**ch**es		
rea**ch**ed		

When a word or syllable beginning with the sound /**iuw**/ follows the sound /**t**/, a /**ch**/ sound is formed.

Listen to the examples and repeat them after the speaker.

EXAMPLES

situation	let you	can't you
ritual	don't you	didn't you
factual	won't you	wouldn't you
congratulations		

Practice for Mastery

Listen to the following sentences featuring the sound /**ch**/, and repeat them after the speaker.

EXAMPLES

The teacher chose Chinese Checkers for the children.
Charles and Chuck lunched on cheese and chips.
Couldn't you eat your lunch, and then watch the match?
Didn't you watch the speech on channel 7?
I can't let you exchange the watch.

About the Letter Combination ch

The letter combination ch is silent in the following word. Listen and repeat.

EXAMPLES

yacht

Introducing the Sound /j/

To make the sound /**j**/, place the center of the tongue against the palate, stop the air completely, then release it abruptly with a voiced sound. (See Figure 28.)

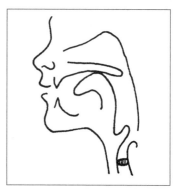

Figure 28.
The sound /j/

EXAMPLES

jam	germ	bridge	soldier
just	gym	judged	
ajar	agency	edges	
major	region		
	huge		

The sound /**d**/ followed by /**iuw**/ is pronounced /**j**/.

Listen to the examples and repeat them after the speaker.

EXAMPLES

education	did you	had you
graduate	would you	
individual	could you	

Practice for Mastery

Listen to the following sentences featuring the sound /**j**/ and then repeat them after the speaker.

EXAMPLES

I wante**d y**ou t**o** come t**o** my gra**du**ati**o**n.

Jim's *a* **j**uni**o**r, ma**jo**ring in e**du**cati**o**n.

Woul**d y**ou please re**gi**ste**r** at the **g**ym?

Jill, in he**r j**eans, **j**umped into he**r j**eep.

Janice, di**d y**ou see the sol**die**r?

UNIT TWENTY-THREE
THE SOUNDS /sh/, /zh/

Introducing the Sound /sh/

To make the sound /**sh**/, touch the palate with the sides of the tongue and release the air slowly through the passageway formed down the center of the tongue. Do not stop the air flow. Do not make a sound with your voice. (See Figure 29.)

Figure 29.
The sound /sh/

Listen to the following examples and repeat them after the speaker.

EXAMPLES

sug*a*r	**sh**ame	ment*io*n	so*ci*al
sure	**sh**oe		spe*ci*al
	fa**sh***io*n	**ch**ef	
a**ss**ure	wi**sh***e*s	**ch**auffeur	oce*a*n
i**ss**ue	wi**sh**ed	m*a***ch**ine	
anx*ious*	ten**s***io*n		

Practice for Mastery

Listen to the following sentences featuring the sound /**sh**/, and repeat them after the speaker.

94

EXAMPLES

> Don't mention her anxious expression.
> Sean assured me he'd shine his shoes.
> Share the sugar with Charlotte.
> She wished she had gone shopping.

Practice in Context

Now say this poem, one line at a time, after the speaker.

Sharon and Charlotte shopped for shallots.
The shallots were shipped from chateaux.
Sharon shared the shallots
That were shipped in the box.
Should she share the champagne, too? No!

Contrasting Sound Practice

To compare /ch/ from Unit Twenty-two with /sh/, repeat the following words after the speaker.

EXAMPLES

/ch/	/sh/	/ch/	/sh/
chin	shin	cheek	chic
cheese	she's	which, witch	wish
choose	shoes	watch	wash
cheap	sheep	watches	washes
chair	share	matching	mashing
chop	shop	matched	mashed
chip	ship	crutch	crush

Recognition Practice

Four sentences are recorded on the CD. Below, circle the ones you hear, then check your work on page 97.

EXERCISE

1. Charles hurt his chin.   Charles hurt his shin.
2. This is your chair.   This is your share.
3. His witches are evil.   His wishes are evil.
4. Will you watch the baby?   Will you wash the baby?

Introducing the Sound /zh/

To make the sound /**zh**/, touch your palate with the sides of your tongue, and release the air slowly through the passage-way formed down the center of the tongue. Do not stop the air. Make a sound with your voice. (See Figure 30.)

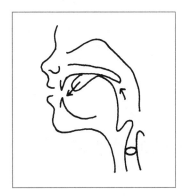

Figure 30.
The sound /zh/

Listen to the following examples and repeat them after the speaker.

a*z*ure	mea*s*ure	A*s*ia	gara*ge*
	u*su*al	vi*si*on	bei*ge*
		Per*si*an	presti*ge*
			re*gi*me
		equa*ti*on	gara*ge*s

This sound does not occur at the beginning of words.

Practice for Mastery

Listen to the following sentences featuring the sound /**zh**/, then repeat them after the speaker.

They u*su*ally watch televi*si*on for plea*s*ure.
She occa*si*onally wears her bei*ge* blouse.
Take th*e* u*su*al mea*s*urements.
They found th*e* trea*s*ure in A*s*ia.

Answers to Exercise

Recognition Practice, p. 96 Charles hurt his shin. This is your chair. His wishes are evil. Will you watch the baby?

UNIT TWENTY-FOUR
THE SOUNDS /s/, /z/

Introducing the Sound /s/

To make the sound /s/, place the center of your tongue against the palate and release the air slowly, but do not stop the air, and do not make a sound with your voice. (See Figure 31.)

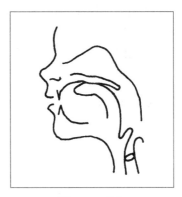

Figure 31.
The sound /s/

Listen to the following examples and repeat the words after the speaker.

EXAMPLES

say	scene	cell
some		recent
square	kiss	acid
small	missed	face
eraser	bosses	
fast		waltz
leased	psychology	waltzed

The letter <u>x</u> is often pronounced as /k/ + /s/.

EXAMPLES

ax	*e*xpect	fix	fox	tuxedo
rela*x*ed	extr*a*			
sax*o*phone	exe*r*cise			

Be careful not to add a vowel sound before the /s/ at the beginning of a word. To avoid this, try pronouncing the /s/ at the end of the previous word.

Listen to the examples and repeat them after the speaker.

EXAMPLES

I s/peak S/pan*i*sh. ("Ice peaks panish.")
Steve s/pends his pennies on s/tamps.
Scott s/kates at *a* s/pe*cia*l s/kating rink.
Stacy s/tays *i*n th*e* S/tates with her s/tepsist*e*r.

Usage Tips

- The final -s of plurals and third person (he, she, it) present tense verb forms is pronounced /s/ when it follows the voiceless consonant sounds /p/, /t/, /k/, /f/, and /θ/.
- The 's indicating possession or a contraction of <u>is</u> or <u>us</u> is also pronounced /s/ when it follows the voiceless consonants.

Listen to the following examples, repeat the words after the speaker, then listen for the confirmation.

EXAMPLES

Noun plurals	3rd-person singular verbs	Possessives and certain contractions
maps	tapes	Pat's
		Jack's
hats	hits	Ruth's
socks	cooks	
beliefs	looks	Miss Crist's
graphs	laughs	
baths		let's (let us)
wasps	grasps	it's (it is)
tests	tastes	that's (that is)
tasks	asks	what's (what is)

Practice for Mastery

Listen to the following sentences featuring the sound /s/, and repeat them after the speaker.

EXAMPLES

Let's sew some snowsuits, said Sally.
The sly fox sits in the forest and waits.
Let's ask the guests for a list of requests.
Miss Smith cooks the best feasts.
Send Sue to the store on Saturday.
Small Stephen still smiles sweetly.
Stephanie slowly spins her sled in the snow.
The Spanish speak Spanish in Spain.
It's the worst snowstorm I've seen.

About the Letter s

The letter s is silent in the following words. Listen, and repeat each word after the speaker.

EXAMPLES

corps	chassis	chamois
aisle	debris	lisle

Contrasting Sound Practice

To compare the sound /**sh**/, from Unit Twenty-three, with /**s**/, repeat the following words.

EXAMPLES

/sh/	/s/	/sh/	/s/
shoot, **ch**ute	**s**uit	**sh**e'll	**s**eal
shed	**s**aid	**sh**ock	**s**ock
shower	**s**our	**sh**ip	**s**ip
shoe	**s**ue	**sh**ine	**s**ign
show	**s**ew, **s**ow, **s**o	**sh**elf	**s**elf
shame	**s**ame	**sh**ave	**s**ave
sheet	**s**eat	lea**sh**	lea**s**e
she'd	**s**eed	me**sh**	me**ss**

Recognition Practice

Four sentences that feature these two sounds are recorded on the CD. Below, circle the ones you hear, then check your answers on page 108.

EXERCISE

1. It was a big shock.   It was a big sock.
2. Can you ship it?   Can you sip it?
3. Can you shave my face?   Can you save my face?
4. They got good sheets.   They got good seats.

Introducing the Sound /z/

To make the /z/ sound, place the center of the tongue against the palate; release the air slowly, without stopping. Make a sound with your voice.

CD 2
TRACK
11

Figure 32.
The sound /z/

Listen to the following examples and repeat the words after the speaker.

EXAMPLES

zero	**x**erox	ea**s**y
la**z**y	**x**ylophone	cou**s**in
free**z**e	an**x**iety	chee**s**e

- The letter <u>x</u> is sometimes pronounced as /g/ + /z/.

EXAMPLES

e**x**amine	e**x**aggerate	e**x**ert
e**x**act	e**x**ist	

Contrasting Sound Practice

Compare the sound /s/ with the sound /z/ by repeating the following words after the speaker.

EXAMPLES

/s/	/z/	/s/	/z/
sip	zip	place	plays
Sue	zoo	cease	sees
loose	lose	raced	raised
rice	rise		

Usage Tip

- The sounds /s/ and /z/ can indicate the difference between a noun and a verb. Repeat the following examples after the speaker.

EXAMPLES

Nouns—/s/	Verbs—/z/
the *a*buse	to *a*buse
the *a*dvice	to *a*dvise
the *e*xcuse	to *e*xcuse
th*e* grease	to grease
th*e* house	to house
th*e* use	to use

Practice for Mastery

Now repeat these sentences after the speaker.

EXAMPLES

We c*a*n house five *o*f y*o*ur guests *a*t our beach house.
There *i*s no use f*o*r that gadg*e*t. I can't use it.
Vict*i*ms *o*f abuse sometimes learn to *a*buse oth*e*rs.
When I asked him for *a*dvice, he *a*dvised me to
keep qui*e*t.
We *e*xcused him that time, but there w*a*s no *e*xcuse for his
behav*i*or.

Usage Tips

- Noun plurals, third person present tense verb forms, possessives, and contractions after vowels and the voiced consonants /b/, /d/, /g/, /v/, /m/, /n/, /ng/, /l/, /r/, and /d/ are spelled -s or -es, and pronounced /z/. Be very careful *not* to pronounce the vowel e between the voiced consonant and s.

Listen to the following examples and repeat them after the speaker.

EXAMPLES

Noun plurals	3rd-person singular verbs
potatoes	cries
labs	sees
heads	does
dogs	rides
leaves	leaves
rooms	breathes
cans	comes
things	runs
prisms	

Possessives	Contractions with is
Bob's	he's
Peg's	she's
Martha's	
his	
hers	
yours	
ours	
theirs	

Listen to the following sentences featuring the sound /z/, and repeat them after the speaker.

> She**'s** my friend**'s** cou*si*n.
> He read**s** newspape*r*s and maga*z*ine**s** on Thursday**s**.
> He love**s** hi**s** new toy**s**.
> Su*s*a n**'s** cou*si*n leave**s** on Wednesday.

- After the sounds /**s**/, /**sh**/, /**z**/, /**zh**/, /**ch**/ and /**j**/, add the unstressed vowel /**ə**/ before the grammatical -**s**. The combined sound /**əz**/ adds one syllable to the word.

Listen to the following examples, repeat them after the speaker, then listen for the confirmation.

Noun plurals	3rd-person singular verbs	Possessives
glass*e*s	kiss*e*s	Bru*ce*'s
wish*e*s	brush*e*s	Trish's
bruis*e*s	prais*e*s	Ros*e*'s
garag*e*s	massag*e*s	Solang*e*'s
church*e*s	match*e*s	Mrs. Gooch's
pag*e*s	stag*e*s	Pag*e*'s

Practice for Mastery

Listen to the following sentences featuring the sound /**əz**/ and repeat them after the speaker.

> He wash*e*s his cars in Charles's garag*e*s.
> She teach*e*s Bru*ce*'s nie*ce*'s friend.
> Ros*e*'s daughte*r* wish*e*s she had new glass*e*s.
> Mrs. Jones fax*e*s pag*e*s of messa*ge*s to our offi*ce*s.
> All of Mrs. Watkins's watch*e*s *a*re Rolex*e*s.

Practice in Context

Listen to the following poems which feature the sounds /s/, /z/, and /əz/, and repeat them line by line during the pauses.

The Supermarket
(Plural Nouns)

What's in the store?
/s/
Carrots, beets,
Grapes, meats,
Drinks, cakes,
Soups, sweets,
Leeks, soaps,
Lots of treats.
/z/
Onions, potatoes,
Cans of tomatoes,
Breads, medicines,
Vegetables, like peas,
Non-food items,
All kinds of cheese.
/əz/
Lettuces, radishes,
Packages, juices,
Peaches, matches,
Good things for all uses,
Spices, low prices,
Some surprises,
No abuses.

The Doll
(Third-person Singular Verbs)

What does she do?

/s/

She laughs, talks,

Wets, walks,

Sleeps, drinks,

Eats, blinks,

And asks for nothing.

/z/

She soothes, cries,

Lies in the crib,

Smiles, sings,

Comfort brings.

/əz/

She dances, entrances,

Amuses, amazes,

And causes no trouble.

The Lost and Found
(Possessives and Contractions)

/s/

Whose coat is this?

It's Jack's or Rick's.

And that one?

That's either Pat's or Mick's.

This hat's pretty,

Is it Miss Smith's?

It looks like the kind

She always picks.

/z/

These shoes are big

They might be John's.

But they could be

His brother Tom's.

Who knows whose things

Are in these rooms?

Those sweaters are probably

Old Ms. Blume's.

/əz/

Galoshes, britches,
sashes, watches,
Are they Rose's,
Or Mrs. Dodge's?
They could be Charles's
Or Mrs. Welsh's,
But they're more likely
Someone else's.

Answers to Exercise

Recognition Practice, p. 101 It was a big shock. Can you sip it? Can you save my face? They got good seats.

Unit Twenty-Five
The Sounds /l/, /r/

Introducing the Sound /l/

To pronounce /l/, curl your tongue up; put the underside of the tongue firmly on the back of your top teeth and make a sound with your voice. (See Figure 33.)

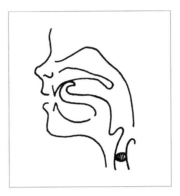

Figure 33.
The sound /l/

Listen to the examples and repeat them after the speaker.

EXAMPLES

lake	daily	clean	male	yellow
love	solve	glass	an*im*al	filled
	shelf	place	alcohol	will
	film			

Usage Tip

- The subject pronouns plus -'**ll** form contractions with the final /l/ sound of <u>will</u>, indicating some instances of future time.

Listen to the examples and repeat them after the speaker.

EXAMPLES

I'll	she'll	we'll
you'll	it'll (it-əl)	they'll
he'll		

Practice for Mastery

Listen to the following sentences featuring the sound /l/, and repeat them after the speaker.

EXAMPLES

Lola likes to laugh a lot.
That fellow, Luke, loves the bowling alley.
She'll like the lovely landscape.
We'll help you fill the glasses.

About the Letter l

The letter l is silent in the following words. Listen, and repeat each word after the speaker.

EXAMPLES

half	could	Lincoln
halves	should	
salve	would	

Introducing the Sound /r/

To make the sound /r/, keep the tongue back; do not let your tongue touch inside your mouth; round your lips and push them forward. Make a voiced sound. (See Figures 34A and 34B.)

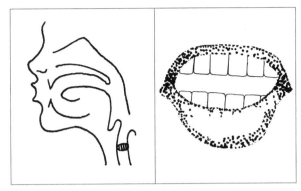

Figures 34A, 34B.
The sound /r/

Listen to the examples and repeat them after the speaker.

EXAMPLES

race	cry	around
ride	draw	carol
	from	
write	green	
	price	
	try	
	through	
mirror	pair	fears
colonel	more	fires
bird	martyr	
orphan		cared
surprise		fired

Usage Tips

- The grammar markers -s and -ed are voiced after /r/.

Listen to the following examples and repeat them after the speaker.

/r/ + /z/	/r/ + /d/
fears	feared
cares	cared
fires	fired
implores	implored
lures	lured

- /r/ plus <u>e</u> is a prefix that indicates "to do again."

Listen to the examples and repeat them after the speaker.

re-do	**re-**decorate
re-peat	**re-**write

- <u>e</u> or <u>o</u> (both pronounced /ə/) plus /r/ is a noun marker meaning "a person who does something."

Listen to the examples and repeat them after the speaker.

teach*er*	sinn*er*	act*or*	exec*u*t*or*
preach*er*	read*er*	doct*or*	
lawy*er*	speed*er*	tut*or*	

- <u>e</u> plus /r/ at the end of an adjective indicates its comparative form.

Listen to the examples and repeat them after the speaker.

EXAMPLES

taller	older	shorter	younger
richer	faster	poorer	slower
sweeter	happier	dearer	sillier
nicer	friendlier	newer	cozier

- **-r** at the end of a pronoun can indicate possession.

Listen to the examples and repeat them after the speaker.

EXAMPLES

your	her
our	their

- **'re** indicates a contraction of the verb <u>are</u>.

Listen to the examples and repeat them after the speaker.

EXAMPLES

you're	they're
we're	there're

Practice for Mastery

Listen to the following sentences featuring the sound /r/ and repeat them after the speaker.

EXAMPLES

Rita read three very short stories.
Roger, the **writ**er, brought thirty red ro**s**es.
Remember to write to your friends.
Robert ran to the store for his mother.
There're prettier flowers at the florist's.
We're here to remember our father.

Contrasting Sound Practice

To compare the sound /l/ with the sound /r/, repeat the following words after the speaker.

EXAMPLES

/l/	/r/
led, lead	red, read
lift	rift
liver	river
laughed	raft
light	right, write
low	row
alive	arrive
believe	bereave
belly	berry
plays	prays, praise
climb	crime
clam	cram
flight	fright
label	labor
pale, pail	pare, pair, pear

Recognition Practice

Ten words featuring /l/ and /r/ sounds are recorded next on the CD. Below, circle the words you hear, then check your answers on page 115.

EXERCISE

1. alive	arrive	6. flight	fright
2. led	red	7. plays	prays
3. climb	crime	8. pail	pair
4. laughed	raft	9. liver	river
5. light	right	10. belly	berry

Recognition Practice

You will hear five sentences on the CD. Circle the ones you hear, then check your answers below.

Exercise

1. Laura prays all day.	Laura plays all day.
2. Please get me a pear.	Please get me a pail.
3. Is it right yet?	Is it light yet?
4. Can you read them?	Can you lead them?
5. The teacher corrected the tests.	The teacher collected the tests.

Practice in Context

Now repeat this poem, one line at a time, to practice /l/ and /r/.

What'll you have?
  I'll have lemon pie, with lots of meringue on the top.
You'll get fat; you'll get sick; you'll be sorry tomorrow.
   Never mind. I'll have diet pop.

Answers to Exercises

Recognition Practice, p. 114 arrive; red; climb; laughed; right; flight; plays; pair, pare, or pear; river; belly

Recognition Practice, Laura plays all day. Please get me a pear. Is it right yet? Can you lead them? The teacher collected the tests.

Unit Twenty-Six
The Sounds /m/, /n/, /ŋ/

Introducing the Sound /m/

To produce the sound /**m**/, press your lips together and make a voiced, humming sound; release the air through your nose. (See Figure 35.)

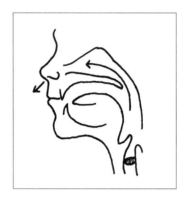

Figure 35.
The sound /m/

Listen to the following examples and repeat them after the speaker.

EXAMPLES

maybe	to**m**orrow	na**m**e	ga**m**es	co**mb**
mother	fa**m**ous	the**m**	ta**m**ed	cli**mb**
		hi**m**	ca**m**p	
		fro**m**		

Usage Tip

- I'**m** = I am. The sound /**m**/ is the contracted verb in the sentence.

116

Practice for Mastery

Listen to the following sentences featuring the sound /**m**/, and repeat them after the speaker.

EXAMPLES

> **My** name is E**m**ily.
> **M**aybe **my m**other will **m**ake something.
> I'**m** coming home with the**m** t**o**morrow.
> **M**y roo**mm**ate's fr**om M**aine.
> I'**m** fr**om** Al**a**bam**a**.

Introducing the Sound /n/

To pronounce /**n**/, place your tongue against your palate and hold it there; make a voiced sound and release the air through your nose. (See Figure 36.)

Figure 36.
The sound /n/

Listen to the examples and repeat them after the speaker.

name	any	and	sane	plains
never	money	angel	then	trained
		interest	envy	
know	funny	thin		

Usage Tips

- **-n** is added to the indefinite article <u>a</u> before words that begin with vowels.

  The sound /**n**/ makes the difference between the articles <u>a</u> and <u>an</u>. The article <u>a</u> is used before words that begin with a consonant sound, while <u>an</u> is used before those that begin with a vowel sound. Listen to the following examples.

Words that begin with a consonant sound	Words that begin with a vowel sound
a hat	*a*n apple
a lock	*a*n orange
a man	*a*n extra copy
a nice man	*a*n inch
a rose	*a*n elevator
a sentence	*a*n umbrella
a xerox copy	*a*n apartment

Most words that begin with the letter <u>h</u> are pronounced with the consonant sound /**h**/, and are preceded by <u>a</u>. Listen to the following examples.

EXAMPLES

> *a* happy child
> *a* hysterical child
> *a* history lesson
> *a* historic house
> *a* historical novel

However, the letter <u>h</u> is silent in a few words that begin with a vowel sound. <u>An</u> is used before these words. Listen to the following examples.

EXAMPLES

> *an* honor
> *an* honest answer
> *an* honorable discharge

The names for the following consonant letters actually begin with vowel sounds.

<u>H</u> (eiych)	<u>L</u> (ɛll)	<u>M</u> (ɛm)	<u>N</u> (ɛn)
<u>R</u> (ar)	<u>S</u> (ɛss)	<u>X</u> (ɛks)	

Use the article <u>an</u> when using these letters by name. Listen to the examples, and repeat them after the speaker.

EXAMPLES

an HOV lane	*an* NBC program	*an* x-ray
an LSAT test	*an* R.S.V.P.	
an MBA degree	*an* S.O.S.	

- **-n't** is added to the verb <u>to be</u> and to auxiliary verbs to make contractions of those verbs and <u>not</u>.

When the **n't** follows the sounds /**d**/ /**t**/ /**v**/ /**s**/ /**z**/, the vowel sound /ə/ and the /**n**/ are pronounced together, adding a syllable to the word. Listen to the examples, and repeat them after the speaker.

One syllable	Two syllables
aren't (arnt)	wouldn't (wud-ənt)
weren't (wernt)	shouldn't (shud-ənt)
don't (dont)	couldn't (cud-ənt)
can't (cant)	didn't (did-ənt)
	hadn't (had-ənt)
	mightn't (maiyt-ənt)
	haven't (have-ənt)
	isn't (is-ənt)
	hasn't (has-ənt)
	wasn't (was-ənt)
	mustn't (mus-ənt)

- *-e*n is the past participle marker for many verbs.

Listen to the examples and repeat them after the speaker.

take**n**	give**n**	froze**n**
eate**n**	gotte**n**	prove**n**
drive**n**		

Practice for Mastery

Listen to the following sentences featuring the sound /**n**/, and repeat them after the speaker.

The*e* sun shines.
The*e* thin man is *a*n Afri*ca*n dance*r*.
Mine is fine.
Tony has take**n** the*e* train.
Nancy has many **n**ew friends.
They have**n't** eate**n** the*e* tun*a*.

About the Letter n

The letter n is silent in the following words. Listen, and repeat each word after the speaker.

EXAMPLES

autumn	column	hymn

Contrasting Sound Practice

To compare /**m**/ with /**n**/, repeat the following words after the speaker.

EXAMPLES

/**m**/	/**n**/	/**m**/	/**n**/
might	**n**ight	he**m**	he**n**
mere	**n**ear	la**m**e	la**n**e
di**m**e	di**n**e	si**mm**er	si**nn**er

Recognition Practice

Four sentences featuring the sounds /**m**/ and /**n**/ are recorded next on the CD. Circle the ones you hear, then check your answers on page 126.

EXERCISE

1. I'm doing the same thing.   I'm doing the sane thing.
2. We would love a   We would love a
   little sum.   little son.
3. She brought a hem   She brought a hen
   for me to fix.   for me to fix.
4. The dimmer's on   The dinner's on
   the table.   the table.

Introducing the Sound /ŋ/

To make the sound /ŋ/, bring the back of your tongue up against the velum, close the air off completely, and release it through the nose. (See Figure 37.)

CD 3
TRACK
3

Figure 37.
The sound /ŋ/

Listen to the examples and repeat them after the speaker.

EXAMPLES

long	hanger	tongue
strong	singer	
singing	belonged	
going	belongings	

A double consonant sound is formed when /**ng**/ is followed by the sounds /**g**/ or /**k**/.

Listen to the examples and repeat them after the speaker.

EXAMPLES

finger	stronger	thanking	sinking
longer	tangle	thinking	drinking

There are three consonant sounds together in the following words. Listen, and repeat them after the speaker.

EXAMPLES

tha**nked**	anx*ious*
(ŋ + k + t)	(ŋ + k + sh)

Usage Tip

- **-ing** is added to the verb to form the present participle.

Listen to the examples and repeat them after the speaker.

EXAMPLES

I'm goi**ng**.
She's looki**ng**.
They were shoppi**ng**.
We have been looki**ng**.
The book is interesti**ng**.
The movie was fascinati**ng**.

Practice for Mastery

Listen to the following sentences featuring the sound /ŋ/ and repeat them after the speaker.

EXAMPLES

The si**ng**er sa**ng** too many lo**ng** so**ng**s.
Your fi**ng**ers are lo**ng**er and stro**ng**er than mine.
The ri**ng**s belo**ng** on the si**ng**er's fi**ng**er.

Contrasting Sound Practice

Now compare the sound /**m**/ with the sound /**ŋ**/ by repeating the following words.

EXAMPLES

/m/	/ŋ/	/m/	/ŋ/
rim	ring	swimmer	swinger
rum	rung	simmer	singer
sum, some	sung	Sam	sang
swim	swing		

Dictation Practice

Listen to the four sentences recorded on the CD and write the ones you hear. Check your answers are on page 126.

EXERCISE

1. He gave me a rim last week.
   He gave me a ring last week.
2. She's dating a swimmer.
   She's dating a swinger.
3. She said she could swim it.
   She said she could swing it.
4. Mama has some good songs.
   Mama has sung good songs.

Contrasting Sound Practice

Compare /n/ and /ŋ/ by repeating the following words after the speaker.

EXAMPLES

/n/	/ŋ/	/n/	/ŋ/
lawn	long	stun	stung
run	rung	thin	thing
fan	fang	sin	sing

Recognition Practice

Below, circle the four sentences you hear on the CD, then check your work on page 126.

EXERCISE

1. It was a lawn party.	It was a long party.
2. It hurts him to sin.	It hurts him to sing.
3. I think she has fans.	I think she has fangs.
4. He has run four times.	He has rung four times.

Contrasting Sound Practice

Compare /m/, /n/, and /ŋ/ by repeating the following words after the speaker.

EXAMPLES

/m/	/n/	/ŋ/
rum	run	rung
Sam	San	sang
simmer	sinner	singer
some	son, sun	sung
whim	win	wing

Practice in Context

Listen to the following dialogue featuring the sounds /m/, /n/, and /ŋ/, and repeat each line after the speakers.

—Sam, how *is* your son?
—He's fine, thanks! You know, he's nineteen now.
—What's he doing?
—He's going to the University of New Mexico and he's planning to be an engineer.
—When *is* he coming home?
—He's coming soon, on the ninth of June.

Answers to Exercises

Recognition Practice, p. 121 I'm doing the sane thing. We would love a little sum. She brought a hem for me to fix. The dimmer's on the table.

Dictation Practice, p. 124 He gave me a rim last week. She's dating a swimmer. She said she could swing it. Mama has sung good songs.

Recognition Practice, p. 125 It was a lawn party. It hurts him to sing. I think she has fans. He has rung four times.

UNIT TWENTY-SEVEN
THE SOUNDS /θ/, /ð/

Introducing the Sound /θ/

To make the sound /θ/, hold the tip of your tongue between your top and bottom teeth; force the air out with a voiceless sound. (See Figure 38.)

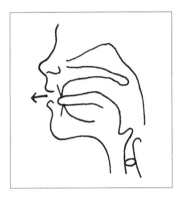

Figure 38.
The sound /θ/

Listen to the following examples and repeat them after the speaker.

EXAMPLES

thank	tru**th**ful	heal**th**	bir**th**s
thing	weal**th**y	tee**th**	dea**th**s
thirsty	no**th**ing	mon**th**	
	some**th**ing		

Usage Tips

- -<u>th</u>, pronounced /θ/, can indicate the noun form of an adjective.

Listen to the next examples and repeat them after the speaker.

width	(wide)	strength	(strong)
depth	(deep)	breadth	(broad)
length	(long)		

- -th , pronounced /θ/, indicates all the ordinal numbers except for first, second, and third, and combinations that end with first, second, and third. It also indicates all fractions except for half and third.

Listen to the following examples and repeat them after the speaker.

fourth	fifteenth	eightieth
fifth	sixteenth	ninetieth
sixth	seventeenth	hundredth
seventh	eighteenth	thousandth
eighth	nineteenth	millionth
ninth	twentieth	
tenth	thirtieth	one-fourth
eleventh	fortieth	three-fifths
twelfth	fiftieth	seven-eighths
thirteenth	sixtieth	
fourteenth	seventieth	

Practice for Mastery

Listen to the following sentences featuring the sound /θ/ and repeat them after the speaker.

EXAMPLES

We bo**th** need some**th**ing for our **th**roats.
He **th**ought **th**irty **th**ousand doll*a*rs w*a*s no**th**ing.
She took *a*n oa**th** t*o* tell th*e* tru**th**.
Thanksgiving is on th*e* four**th** **Th**ursday *o*f th*e* mon**th** *o*f November.
Ma**th**ematics is one *o*f her streng**th**s.
He may be weal**th**y, but he's ru**th**less and uncou**th**.

Contrasting Sound Practice

Compare the sound /s/, from Unit Twenty-four, with the sound /θ/ by repeating the following words after the speaker.

EXAMPLES

/s/	/θ/	/s/	/θ/
sin	thin	miss	myth
sing	thing	mass	math
sink	think	pass	path
sought	thought	mouse	mouth
sank	thank	force	forth, fourth
sum	thumb	truce	truth
seem, seam	theme		

Recognition Practice

Four sentences featuring the sounds /s/ and /θ/ are recorded next on the CD. Below, circle the ones you hear, then check your answers on page 132.

1. The truce is important.	The truth is important.
2. I sought it out.	I thought it out.
3. He can't find the pass.	He can't find the path.
4. Show the teacher your seam.	Show the teacher your theme.

Introducing the Sound /ð/

To pronounce /ð/, hold the tip of your tongue between your top and bottom teeth; release the air with a voiced sound. (See Figure 39.)

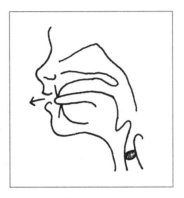

Figure 39.
The sound /ð/

Listen to the following examples and repeat them after the speaker.

EXAMPLES

they	lather	bathe	bathes
these	together	clothe	clothes
those	breathing	breathe	soothed
the	rhythm		

Practice for Mastery

Listen to the following sentences featuring the consonant /ð/, and repeat them after the speaker.

EXAMPLES

> **Th**e mother soothed **th**e teething baby.
> My bro**th**er loathes **th**is wea**th**er.
> Fa**th**er seethed when he saw **th**ese lea**th**er pants.

About the Letters <u>th</u>

The letters <u>th</u> are silent in the following words. Listen, and repeat each word after the speaker.

EXAMPLES

> asthm*a*   isthm*us*

Contrasting Sound Practice

Now compare the sound /**d**/, from Unit Nineteen, with the sound /**ð**/. Repeat the words after the speaker.

EXAMPLES

/**d**/	/**ð**/
dare	**th**ere, **th**eir, **th**ey're
dough	**th**ough
den	**th**en
la**dd**er	la**th**er
we**tt**er	wea**th**er, whe**th**er
le**tt**er	lea**th**er
u**tt**er, u**dd**er	o**th**er
fo**dd**er	fa**th**er
mu**tt**er	mo**th**er
wri**t**ing, ri**d**ing	wri**th**ing
bree**d**	brea**th**e
sue**d**	soo**th**e
see**d**	see**th**e
ska**t**ing	sca**th**ing

Recognition Practice

Listen carefully to the following four sentences on the CD, and circle below the ones you hear. Check your work below.

EXERCISE

1. Did you see the letter?   Did you see the leather?
2. He made a big ladder.   He made a big lather.
3. Yes, they sued him.   Yes, they soothe him.
4. It was his mutter   It was his mother
   that bothered her.   that bothered her.

Answers to Exercises

Recognition Practice, p. 130 The truce is important. I sought it out. He can't find the path. Show the teacher your seam.

Recognition Practice, Did you see the letter? He made a big ladder. Yes, they soothe him. It was his mutter that bothered her.

Unit Twenty-Eight
The Sound /h/

Introducing the Sound /h/

To make the sound /**h**/, keep your tongue free and force air from the throat with a voiceless sound. (See Figure 40.)

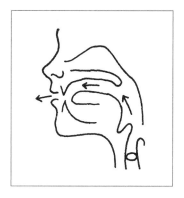

Figure 40.
The sound /h/

Listen to the examples and repeat them after the speaker.

EXAMPLES

hay	ma**h**oga ny	w**h**o
hill	O**h**io	w**h**ole
hope	alco**h**ol	
huge	pre**h**eat	
hurry		

When the words <u>he</u>, <u>her</u>, <u>his</u>, <u>him</u>, and <u>has</u> are unstressed, the /**h**/ sound is often not pronounced.

Listen to the examples, and repeat them after the speaker.

EXAMPLES

I don't know where (h)e is.
He gave it to (h)er yesterday.
I haven't seen (h)im.

133

Practice for Mastery

Listen to the following sentences and repeat them after the speaker.

Examples

> Does (h)e have any hope?
> Hi! What's your hurry?
> Howard is hiding in Ohio.
> They have a huge hotel at Lake Tahoe.
> Her husband brought home a huge mahogany hutch.

About the Letter h

The letter h is silent in the following examples. Listen, and repeat each word after the speaker.

Examples

honor, honest	vehement
herb	exhaust
heir	exhort
hour	exhume
	shepherd
John	what
oh, ah	when
night, fight, etc.	where
though, through, etc.	why
caught, bought, etc.	khaki
	rhythm
	thyme

Unit Twenty-Nine
The Sounds /w/, /y/

Introducing the Sound /w/

To make the sound /**w**/, relax your tongue, then round your lips and press them back against the front of your teeth. Make a sound as you release your lips. (See Figure 41.)

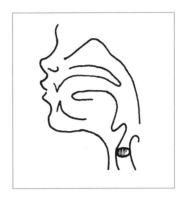

Figure 41.
The sound /w/

Listen to the examples and repeat them after the speaker.

EXAMPLES

way	*a***w**ay	q**u**een
was		
		s**w**eet
		t**w**enty
where	*a***wh**ile	**o**ne
why		**o**nce
whistl*e* (əl)		

135

Practice for Mastery

Listen to the following sentences featuring the sound /**w**/, and repeat them after the speaker.

EXAMPLES

When **w**ill **w**e go *a***w**ay?
The **w**ind **wh**istled in the **w**oods.
D**w**ight *a*nd D**u**ane **w**ent to G**u**am.
Why **w**as there *a* **w**ar?
One of the t**w**ins **w**alked t**w**enty miles.
Wand*a* **w**ore he**r wh**ite dress on **W**ednesday.
I **w**ent fo**r** *a* **w**alk **w**ith **W**alte**r** McGuire.

About the Letter <u>w</u>

The letter <u>w</u> is silent in the following words. Listen, and repeat each word after the speaker.

EXAMPLES

who, whom, whose, whole	two
wren, write, wrong	toward
sword	knowledge

Practice in Context

Repeat this poem after the speaker, one line at a time, to practice /**w**/.

Why do we have an <u>h</u> in *why*,
 and *where, when, what,* *a*nd *white*?
Well, there's *a* <u>w</u> in *who, whose,* *a*nd *whole,*
 and *write* when the meaning is right.

Contrasting Sound Practice

Compare the sound /**v**/, from Unit Twenty-one, with the sound /**w**/, by repeating the following words after the speaker.

EXAMPLES

/v/	/w/	/v/	/w/
vine	wine	vow	wow
very, vary	wary	vile	while
veal	wheel, we'll	veer	we're
vent	went	vest	west
vase	ways, weighs		

Recognition Practice

Four sentences featuring the previous sounds /**v**/ and /**w**/ are recorded next on the CD. Below, circle the ones you hear, then check your answers on page 140.

EXERCISE

1. He took the veal.   He took the wheel.
2. It's in the vest.   It's in the west.
3. What's the vine like?   What's the wine like?
4. Veer to the left.   We're to the left.

Introducing the Sound /y/

To pronounce /**y**/, spread your tongue flat and toward the back of your mouth; do not let your tongue touch the palate. Next, make a wide smile with your lips and bring your tongue forward with a voiced sound. (See Figure 42.)

Figure 42.
The sound /y/

Listen to the following examples and repeat them after the speaker.

yes	**y**et	ma**y**or	iron (ai-**y**ern)
yellow	**y**ear	be**y**ond	

When the sound /**y**/ is followed by the vowel sound /**u**/, the combination is exactly the same as the vowel sound /**iuw**/.

Listen to the examples and repeat them after the speaker.

you	**y**outh	**u**se	**U**tah	us**u**al

Practice for Mastery

Listen to the following sentences featuring the sound /**y**/, and repeat them after the speakers.

EXAMPLES

> May I use **yo**ur iron?
> **Y**es, **y**ou may use it any time.
> He's **a** pop**u**lar hockey pla**y**er at th**e** un**i**versity this **y**ear.
> Th**e** Miami law**y**er w**a**s triumph**a**nt **y**esterday.

About the Letter y

The letter y is silent in the following words. Listen, and repeat each word after the speaker.

EXAMPLES

says	prayers

Contrasting Sound Practice

Compare the sound /**j**/ from Unit Twenty-two, with the sound /**y**/ by repeating the following words.

EXAMPLES

/**j**/	/**y**/	/**j**/	/**y**/
jeer	**y**ear	**j**oke	**y**oke
jello	**y**ellow	**j**et	**y**et
ma**j**or	ma**y**or	**g**el	**y**ell
jam	**y**am	**j**ot	**y**acht

Recognition Practice

Four sentences using the sounds /**j**/ and /**y**/ are recorded next on the CD. Circle the ones you hear and check your answers on page 140.

1. There's no juice.   There's no use.
2. My uncle is the major.   My uncle is the mayor.
3. Has he come by jet?   Has he come by yet?
4. Are you going to jail?   Are you going to Yale?

Practice in Context

Now, repeat the following poem after the speaker, one line at a time, to practice /**j**/ and /**y**/.

> Jeremy bought *a* yellow jet,
> And then he got *a* yacht.
> "Why did you get th*e* yacht," asked Brett,
> "When you hav*e*n't used th*e* yellow jet yet?"

Answers to Exercises

Recognition Practice, p. 137 He took the wheel. It's in the vest. What's the wine like? We're to the left.

Recognition Practice, p. 140 There's no use. My uncle is the major. Has he come by yet? Are you going to jail?

Unit Thirty
Double Consonants

Sometimes a word ending in a consonant sound is followed by a word beginning with the same consonant sound, or one formed in the same position. To pronounce these "double consonants," do not release the sound between words. Emphasize the sound by holding it a little longer.

Listen to the following examples, and repeat them after the speaker.

EXAMPLES

/p/ + /p/	Keep practicing
/b/ + /b/	Grab Brian's hand.
/p/ + /b/	That pup belongs to her.
/t/ + /t/	It's not too much.
/d/ + /d/	Dad didn't tell me.
/t/ + /d/	Don't do that.
/k/ + /k/	I like candy.
/g/ + /g/	That rug goes here.
/k/ + /g/	They like green apples.
/f/ + /f/	Keep off Freddie's flowers.
/v/ + /v/	I love Vermont.
/v/ + /f/	He has lots of friends.
/s/ + /s/	That's scary.
/z/ + /z/	His zeroes are in the wrong place.
/z/ + /s/	His science class is interesting.
/l/ + /l/	He'll like it.
/r/ + /r/	They are wrong.
/m/ + /m/	We named him Mike.
/n/ + /n/	Dan knows the truth.
/θ/ + /θ/	Are you going with three bags?
/θ/ + /ð/	He left with the dog.

There are two exceptions to this pattern. The sounds /ch/ and /j/ must be released before pronouncing another word.

Listen to the examples and repeat them after the speaker.

EXAMPLES

/ch/ + /ch/	I can't rea**ch Ch**arles.
/j/ + /j/	Will you jud**ge Ja**ck's team?
/ch/ + /j/	She's going to tea**ch g**eometry.

Part Three

Stress Patterns

English words can be divided into syllables. Each spoken vowel sound makes one syllable. A syllable can be

- a vowel sound alone,
- a vowel before a consonant,
- a vowel after a consonant, or
- a vowel between consonants.

Unit Thirty-One
Syllables and Stress

Listen to these examples of one-syllable words and repeat them after the speaker.

EXAMPLES

Vowel alone	oh	I	
Vowel-consonant	on	ice	
Consonant-vowel	to	be	you
Consonant-vowel-consonant	big	tough	cute

Each syllable in a word has a degree of emphasis, called stress. There are three stress levels in English, primary (*/*), secondary (*/*), and unstressed (–).

Each word of two or more syllables has one syllable that is longer and louder than the others. It has primary stress. In the examples that follow, these syllables are represented in **extra bold letters**.

Some words and syllables have secondary stress, which is slightly weaker than the primary one, but louder and longer than an unstressed one. These syllables are represented in **bold letters** in the examples.

There are many unstressed syllables in English. They have a short, soft vowel sound and may be difficult to hear at first. They are represented in the examples in Roman type. Unstressed vowels pronounced /ə/ are in *light blue italics.* Be careful to emphasize any consonants that occur with unstressed vowels.

Unit Thirty-Two
Two-Syllable Words

Introducing Primary Stress

A word with two vowel sounds has two syllables. One syllable has primary stress. Say it a little louder and longer than the other. Pronounce the vowel with importance.

The vowel of the unstressed syllable is usually pronounced /ə/, no matter how it is spelled. Make the vowel sound short. Pronounce the consonant sounds clearly and distinctly.

Listen to the following examples and repeat them after the speaker.

EXAMPLES

Primary stress on first syllable		Primary stress on second syllable	
/	–	–	**/**
cli-	*m*ate	*ad-*	**vice**
ac-	*to*r	*ex-*	**cite**
pleas-	*u*re	*con-*	**fused**
sol-	*di*er	*sup-*	**pose**
danc-	*e*s	*sur-*	**prised**
wash-	*e*s		
watch-	*e*s		
fold-	*e*d		
seat-	*e*d		

The sounds /iy/, /ow/, /iuw/, and /ɪ/ often keep their normal pronunciations in unstressed syllables.

Listen to the following examples and repeat them after the speaker.

EXAMPLES

Stress on first syllable		Stress on second syllable	
/	**–**	**–**	**/**
/iy/			
ar-	my	re-	**peat**
ba-	by	de-	**duct**
ci-	ty	be-	**gin**
/ow/			
ar-	row	o-	**bey**
el-	bow	o-	**mit**
fol-	low	o-	**kay**
/iuw/			
ar-	gue	u-	**nique**
neph-	ew		
val-	ue		
/ɪ/			
build-	ing	in-	**stead**
den-	tist	in-	**sist**
mu-	sic	im-	**mune**

Usage Tip

- The stress patterns **/** – and – **/** indicate the difference between certain nouns and verbs.

Listen to the following examples and repeat them after the speaker.

EXAMPLES

Nouns		Verbs	
/	**–**	**–**	**/**
pres-	ent	pre-	**sent**
reb-	el	re-	**bel**
ob-	ject	ob-	**ject**
prog-	ress	pro-	**gress**
rec-	ord	re-	**cord**

To practice the difference in stress between nouns and verbs, repeat the following sentences after the speaker.

EXAMPLES

> We're going to pr**esent** him with a **pres**ent at the reception.
> His brother is a **reb**el. He r**ebels** against all the established rules.
> If you don't **ob**ject, I will put several **obj**ects on the table.
> "When did you r**ecord** your last **rec**ord?," the boy asked the singer.

Introducing Secondary Stress

Some two-syllable words have **primary** stress on the first syllable and **secondary** stress on the second syllable. Say the first syllable strongly. Emphasize the second syllable a little less, but say it with a clear vowel.

CD 3 TRACK 10

Listen to the examples and repeat them after the speaker.

EXAMPLES

/	**/**
ac-	**cent**
ath-	**lete**
fe-	**male**
in-	**come**
in-	**sect**
trans-	**fer**

Usage Tips

- The stress pattern **/** / is common for compound words.

Listen to the examples and repeat them after the speaker.

EXAMPLES

Nouns		Verbs		Adjectives	
/	/	/	/	/	/
air-	plane	dry-	clean	bare-	foot
bird-	house	black-	mail	care-	free
black-	board	brain-	wash	fore-	most
drug-	store	down-	grade	home-	sick
hot-	dog	foot-	note	new-	born
land-	lord	kid-	nap		
make-	up				
rail-	road				

- The stress patterns **/ /** and **– /** indicate the differences between some nouns and verbs.

Listen to the examples and repeat them after the speaker.

EXAMPLES

Nouns		Verbs	
/	/	–	/
com-	bine	com-	**bine**
com-	pact	com-	**pact**
con-	duct	con-	**duct**
con-	flict	con-	**flict**
con-	tract	con-	**tract**
con-	trast	con-	**trast**
con-	vert	con-	**vert**
dis-	count	dis-	**count**
per-	mit	per-	**mit**
pro-	test	pro-	**test**
sus-	pect	sus-	**pect**

Now repeat these sentences to practice the noun-verb differences in stress.

EXAMPLES

> The student's **con**duct was unacceptable.
> The teacher had to co**nduct** him to the principal.
> We signed a **con**tract to buy the house.
> Now we have to co**ntract** an architect to remodel it.
> The young boy's father wouldn't pe**rmit** him to get a
> driver's **per**mit.
> I su**spect** he is one of the **sus**pects.

- The stress patterns **/ /** and **/** – are important for distinguishing the "teen" numbers from the "tens." Note also that they have different pronunciations of the letter t̲.

Listen to the next examples and repeat them after the speaker.

EXAMPLES

Teens		Tens	
/	/	**/**	–
thir-	teen	**thir-**	ty
four-	teen	**for-**	ty
fif-	teen	**fif-**	ty
six-	teen	**six-**	ty
eigh-	teen	**eigh-**	ty
nine-	teen	**nine-**	ty
Seve̲nteen and seve̲nty have an additional unstressed syllable:			
sev ‌ℰn teen		**sev** en ty	

Say the following poem, one line at a time, after the speaker, to practice the tens and teens.

EXAMPLES

> Have you seen my teen?
> She's *a* high school queen
> Be tween sixteen *a*nd seve nteen.
> She c*a*n be flirty, act like thirty,
> Or *a* baby, then *a* lady,
> She makes he r mothe r feel like eighty,
> Or eighteen.

- The stress patterns **/ /** and **/ /** distinguish compound words from other modified nouns.

Listen to the examples that follow and repeat them after the speaker.

EXAMPLES

Compound word / /		Modifier + noun / /	
greenhouse		green	house
bluebird		blue	bird
darkroom		dark	room
hotdog		hot	dog
blackboard		black	board

Listen to these sentences, which compare compound nouns with other modified nouns, and repeat them after the speaker.

EXAMPLES

The kitchen was a **dark room**.
There was a **dark**room in the basement for photos.
I saw a **blue bird** in the yard.
I don't think it was a **blue**bird.
They bought a **new house** with a **green**house and a **bird**bath in the back.

I live in a **white house**, but it's not The **White** House.
He said a few **cross words** when he couldn't finish the **cross**word puzzle.
It was 100°, and Rover was one **hot dog**.
Hot dogs are great at baseball games.

- Some words have secondary stress on the first syllable, and primary on the second.

Listen to the examples and repeat them after the speaker.

EXAMPLES

/	**/**	/	**/**
car-	**toon**	un-	**do**
cash-	**ier**	un-	**pack**
Chin-	**ese**	up-	**date**
post-	**pone**	with-	**draw**

- Verbs with the prefix <u>re</u>, when it means "to do again," also have / **/** as a stress pattern.

Listen to the examples and repeat them after the speaker.

EXAMPLES

/	**/**	/	**/**	/	**/**
re-	**build**	re-	**play**	re-	**wind**
re-	**do**	re-	**set**	re-	**word**
re-	**check**	re-	**tell**	re-	**write**
re-	**heat**	re-	**think**		

- Some verbs followed by prepositions have special meanings, and are called <u>two-word</u> <u>verbs</u> or <u>phrasal</u> <u>verbs</u>. They too have the / **/** stress pattern.

Listen to the examples and repeat them after the speaker.

EXAMPLES

/	**/**	/	**/**	/	**/**
back	**up**	find	**out**	put	**off**
back	**down**	give	**back**	slow	**down**
back	**off**	give	**in**	take	**in**
call	**off**	give	**up**	take	**out**
calm	**down**	hand	**in**	take	**off**
clean	**up**	hand	**out**	use	**up**
dream	**up**	leave	**out**	wind	**up**
dress	**up**	put	**on**		

Practice for Mastery

Now repeat the following sentences featuring the / **/** stress pattern.

After we **unpack**, we'll play Chinese checkers.

I'm going to the cashier to **withdraw** the money.

She will **rewind** the **cartoon** for you.

We'll **retest** your blood **and postpone** your routine exam.

Please slow down, or we'll **wind up** on the side of the road.

Let's find out if we can **take off** next week.

I'll **call off** the next party if you don't **clean up** after this one.

Unit Thirty-Three
Words with Three
or More Syllables

Words with three or more syllables have one syllable with primary stress. The other syllables are either all unstressed, or one has secondary stress and the rest are unstressed.

Introducing Stress Pattern 1

Primary stress is on the first syllable and all other syllables are unstressed.

Listen to these examples of three-syllable words and repeat them after the speaker.

EXAMPLES

/	–	–	**/**	–	–
a-	ni-	mal	**fin-**	ish-	es
cho-	co-	late	**vis-**	i-	ted
fur-	ni-	ture	**vis-**	i-	tor
hos-	pi-	tal	**dir-**	ti-	er
vege-	ta-	ble	**bus-**	i-	est
vis-	it-	ing	**care-**	ful-	ly
or-	ang	-es			

Listen to the following examples of four-syllable words with pattern 1, and repeat them after the speaker.

EXAMPLES

/	–	–	–	**/**	–	–	–
for-	tu-	nate-	ly	**per-**	man-	ent-	ly
in-	no-	cent-	ly	**ser-**	i-	ous-	ly

154

Introducing Stress Pattern 2

Primary stress is on the second syllable and all other syllables are unstressed.

Listen to the following examples of three-syllable words and repeat them after the speaker.

EXAMPLES

–	/	–		–	/	–
a-	**part-**	ment		ex-	**am-**	ple
ba-	**na-**	na		pro-	**hi-**	bit
con-	**di-**	tion		to-	**ge-**	ther
de-	**ci-**	sion				

Next, listen to examples of four-syllable words with pattern 2, and repeat them after the speaker.

EXAMPLES

–	/	–	–		–	/	–	–
com-	**mu-**	ni-	ty		o-	**ri-**	gin-	al
e-	**mer-**	gen-	cy		me-	**chan-**	i-	cal
ex-	**per-**	i-	ence		se-	**cu-**	ri-	ty
in-	**fer-**	i-	or					

Following are some five-syllable words with pattern 2. Repeat them after the speaker.

EXAMPLES

–	/	–	–	–
af-	**fec-**	tion-	ate-	ly
con-	**si-**	der-	a-	ble
con-	**di-**	tion-	al-	ly
co-	**op-**	er-	a-	tive
in-	**ev-**	it-	a-	ble
pro-	**fes-**	sion-	al-	ly

Introducing Stress Pattern 3

Primary stress is on the first syllable and secondary stress is on the third syllable. All other syllables are unstressed.

Listen to some examples of three-syllable words with pattern 3, and repeat them after the speaker.

EXAMPLES

/	**–**	**/**	**/**	**–**	**/**
al-	pha-	**bet**	**pho-**	to-	**graph**
bas-	ket-	**ball**	**qual-**	i-	**fy**
cat-	a-	**logue**	**re-**	cog-	**nize**
en-	ve-	**lope**	**ta-**	ble-	**cloth**
ex-	er-	**cise**	**tel-**	e-	**phone**
grad-	u-	**ate** (verb form)	**thun-**	der-	**storm**
hol-	i-	**day**			

Following are examples of four-syllable words with pattern 3. Repeat them after the speaker.

EXAMPLES

/	**–**	**/**	**–**	**/**	**–**	**/**	**–**
dic-	tion-	**a-**	ry	**or-**	din-	**a-**	ry
com-	pli-	**ca-**	ted	**tel-**	e-	**vi-**	sion
el-	e-	**va-**	tor				

Introducing Stress Pattern 4

Primary stress is on the second syllable and secondary stress is on the fourth syllable. All other syllables are unstressed.

Listen to the next examples of words with pattern 4, and repeat them after the speaker.

EXAMPLES

–	/	–	/		–	/	–	/
a-	**pol-**	*o-*	**gize**		con-	**grat-**	*u-*	**late**
ap-	**pre-**	ci-	**ate**		*par-*	**ti-**	c*i*-	**pate**

Introducing Stress Pattern 5

Secondary stress is on the first syllable and primary stress is on the second syllable. The other syllables are unstressed.

Listen to the following examples of words with pattern 5 and repeat them after the speaker.

EXAMPLES

/	/	–		/	/	–
ath-	**let-**	ic		trans-	**par-**	ent
beau-	**ti-**	c*ian*		um-	**brel-**	l*a*
out-	**stand-**	ing		va-	**ca-**	tion

Introducing Stress Pattern 6

Secondary stress is on the first syllable and primary stress is on the third syllable. All other syllables are unstressed.

Listen to the following examples of three-syllable words with pattern 6 and repeat them after the speaker.

EXAMPLES

/	–	/		/	–	/
af-	ter-	**noon**		gas-	*o-*	**line**
dis-	*ap-*	**pear**		Jap-	*a-*	**nese**
auc-	tion-	**eer**		pi-	*o-*	**neer**
en-	g*i*-	**neer**		un-	der-	**stand**

Now listen to these four-syllable words that have pattern 6. Repeat them after the speaker.

EXAMPLES

/	–	/	–
ad-	ver-	**tise-**	ment
ap-	pli-	**ca-**	tion
ar-	ti-	**fi-**	cial
ce-	le-	**bra-**	tion
dec-	o-	**ra-**	tion
e-	co-	**nom-**	ics
ed-	u-	**ca-**	tion
in-	de-	**pen-**	dence
man-	u-	**fac-**	ture
u-	ni-	**ver-**	sal

UNIT THIRTY-FOUR
ONE SYLLABLE PREFIXES

Prefixes are one- or two-syllable additions that occur at the beginning of some words. They carry certain meanings that modify the words.

The following examples contain one-syllable prefixes that are usually unstressed. Listen to the words and repeat them after the speaker.

EXAMPLES

Prefix					General meaning of prefix
co-	co-	**op-**	*er-*	**ate**	with
con-	con-	**tin-**	ue		with
com-	com-	**mit-**	tee		with
de-	de-	**liv-**	*er*		down, from
dis-	dis-	**cuss**			negative
ex-	ex-	**hib-**	*it*		out, from
mis-	mis-	**take**			wrong
pre-	pre-	**pare**			before
pro-	pro-	**test**			for
re-	re-	**ward**			back

Other one-syllable prefixes usually have secondary stress. Listen and repeat after the speaker.

EXAMPLES

Prefix						General meaning of prefix
bi-	**bi-**	**o-**	lo-	gy		two
in-	**in-**	**ept**				not
ir-	**ir-**	res-	**pon-**	si-	ble	not
mal-	**mal-**	**nour-**	ish			badly
non-	**non-**	**poi-**	son-	ous		not
pan-	**pan-**	o-	**ra-**	ma		all
post-	**post-**	**pone**				after
re-	**re-**	**write**				again
sub-	**sub-**	**let**				under
trans-	**trans-**	**fer**				across
un-	**un-**	**hap-**	py			not
vice-	**vice-**	**pres-**	i-	dent		deputy

UNIT THIRTY-FIVE
TWO-SYLLABLE PREFIXES

As mentioned in the preceding unit, there are prefixes that have two syllables. Here are some examples:

EXAMPLES

Prefix	General meaning
ante-	before
anti-	against
auto-	self
circum-	around
counter-	opposite to
hyper-	more than normal
hypo-	less than normal
inter-	between
micro-	tiny
mono-	one
multi-	many
poly-	many
uni-	one
ultra-	extreme

When these prefixes form a three-syllable word, there is usually primary stress on the first syllable, followed by an unstressed syllable and secondary stress on the third syllable.

Repeat the following examples after the speaker.

EXAMPLES

/	–	/	/	–	/
an-	te-	**date**	**mi-**	cro-	**scope**
an-	ti-	**freeze**	**mon-**	o-	**rail**
au-	to-	**mat**	**mul-**	ti-	**ply**
cir-	cum-	**cize**	**u-**	ni-	**verse**
coun-	ter-	**point**	**ul-**	tra-	**sound**

When two-syllable prefixes form a word of four or more syllables, there is usually secondary stress on the first syllable, no stress on the second, and primary stress on the third. The remaining syllables are unstressed.

Listen carefully and repeat the next examples after the speaker.

EXAMPLES

/	–	/	–	–
an-	te-	**ce-**	dent	
an-	ti-	**so-**	*ci*al	
au-	to-	**ma-**	*ti*c	
cir-	*cu*m-	**ven-**	*ti*on	
coun-	ter-	**clock-**	wise	
hy-	per-	**ac-**	*ti*ve	
hy-	po-	**der-**	*mi*c	
in-	ter-	**ac-**	*ti*on	
mi-	cro-	**sco-**	*pi*c	
mon-	o-	**lin-**	*gu*al	
po-	ly-	**es-**	ter	
u-	*ni*	**ver-**	*sa*l	
mul-	ti-	**na-**	tion-	*a*l
ul-	tra-	**vi-**	o-	let

Some exceptions to this pattern are as follows. Listen, then repeat after the speaker.

EXAMPLES

/	–	–	/
au-	to-	mo-	**bile**

/	/	–	–		/	/	–	–
an-	**ti-**	*ci*-	pate		**mo-**	**nop-**	*o*-	ly
an-	**ti-**	*pa*-	thy		**mo-**	**nog-**	*a*-	m*ou*s
an-	**tiq-**	*ui*-	ty		**mo-**	**not-**	*o*-	ny
an-	**tith-**	*e*-	*si*s					

Unit Thirty-Six
Suffixes

Suffixes are additions of one or more syllables that may be attached to the end of words. They usually have a grammatical function. For example, they can change the part of speech of a basic word, change the tense of a verb, and change the form of an adjective.

It is important to pronounce suffixes clearly, with the proper stress. They are almost always unstressed: Say the vowel sound quickly and with your mouth almost closed, but pronounce the consonant sounds in these syllables distinctly.

After the speaker, repeat the following words that end in unstressed one-syllable suffixes.

EXAMPLES

Noun suffixes		–
-ance	im-**por-**	t*a*nce
-ant	im-**por-**	t*a*nt
-ate	**grad-**u-	*a*te
-ee	em-**ploy-**	ee
-ence	oc-**cur-**	rence
-ent	**cur-**	rent
-er	**driv-**	er
-ist	**so-***c*ial-	ist
-ment	**gov-***e*rn-	ment
-sion	ex-**pan-**	s*io*n
-some	**hand-**	some
-tion	*a*t-**ten-**	t*io*n

Adjective suffixes		_
-al	**mu**-si-	c*a*l
-ent	**cur-**	r*e*nt
-er	**brav-**	*e*r
-est	**brav-**	*e*st
-ful	**help-**	f*u*l
-ic	au-t*o*-**mat-**	ic
-ive	*e*x-**ces-**	s*i*ve
-le	**mul**-ti-	pl*e*
-ous	**jeal-**	*ou*s

Verb suffixes		_
-ed	**want-**	*e*d
-es	**us-**	*e*s
-ing	**read-**	ing

Adverb suffixes		_			_
-ly	**slow-**	ly	**hap**	p*i*	ly
			rap	*i*d	ly

The following one-syllable suffixes are exceptions to the un-stressed pattern. They have secondary stress. Repeat them after the speaker.

Noun suffixes	/	_	/
-day	**hol-**	*i*-	**day**
-graph	**phot-**	*o*-	**graph**
-tude	**at-**	t*i*-	**tude**

EXAMPLES

Verb suffixes			
	/	**–**	**/**
-ate	**grad-**	u-	**ate**
-fy	**qual-**	i-	**fy**
-ize	**crit-**	i-	**cize**

The noun suffix **-eer** has primary stress.

Repeat the next example after the speaker.

EXAMPLES

/	**–**	**/**	**/**	**–**	**/**
pi-	o-	**neer**	rac-	ke-	**teer**
			auc-	tio-	**neer**

The adjective suffix **-ese** has primary stress.

Repeat the example after the speaker.

EXAMPLES

/	**–**	**/**	**/**	**–**	**/**
Jap-	a-	**nese**	Le-	ba-	**nese**
			Su-	da-	**nese**

Some suffixes have two syllables. Both are unstressed.

Repeat the following examples after the speaker.

EXAMPLES

Noun suffixes			
		–	**–**
-ator	**sen-**	a-	tor
-apher	ste-**nog-**	ra-	pher
-eter	ther-**mom-**	e-	ter
-ison	**u-**	ni-	son
-ity	na-tion-**al-**	i-	ty
-ogy	bi-**o-**	lo-	gy

Adjective suffixes		–	–
-able	**ca-**	p*a*-	bl*e*
-ian	C*a*-**na-**	di-	*a*n
-ible	**sen-**	s*i*-	bl*e*
-ical	**rad-**	*i*-	c*a*l
-ier	**pret-**	ti-	*e*r
-iest	**sil-**	li-	*e*st
-ior	su-**pe-**	ri-	or
-ory	**sen-**	s*o*-	ry

Adverb suffixes		–	–
-ally	**prac-**ti-	c*a*l-	ly
-ately	**pri-**	v*a*te-	ly
-ently	**per-**m*a*-	n*e*nt-	ly
-ively	c*o*m-**pe**-t*i*-	t*i*ve-	ly
-ously	**ser-**i-	*o*us-	ly

The following two examples are exceptions to the pattern. They have primary stress on the first syllable of the suffix. Listen and repeat the words after the speaker.

	/
(noun suffix)	**for-ma-**t*i*on
	/
(adverb suffix)	e-v*i*-**dent-**ly

Now repeat the following nouns that have secondary stress on the first syllable of the suffix.

EXAMPLES

/	–	/	–
in-	v*en*-	**to-**	ry
dic-		**ta-**	t*o*r
me-	di-	**a-**	t*o*r
so-	c*ia*-	**lis-**	*m*

Some suffixes may cause the stress of the basic word form to shift to another syllable. Repeat the examples after the speaker.

EXAMPLES

– / – –	– – – / –	
a-**pol**-*o*-gy	*a*-pol-*o*-**get**-ic	
/ – –	– – / – –	
cu-ri-*ou*s	cu-ri-**os**-*i*-ty	
– / – –	– – / –	
e-**con**-*o*-my	ec-*o*-**nom**-ics	
/ – –	– / –	
i-r*o*-ny	i-**ron**-ic	
– / – –	– – – / –	
n*e*-**go**-ti-ate	n*e*-go-ti-**a**-t*io*n	
/ – /	– / – –	– / – –
pho-t*o*-**graph**	pho-**tog**-r*a*-ph*e*r	ph*o*-**tog**-r*a*-phy
/ – –	/ – / –	
pol-*i*-tics	**pol**-*i*-**ti**-c*ia*n	
/ –	– – / –	/ / – –
pub-lic	pub-l*i*-**ca**-t*io*n	**pub**-**lic**-*i*-ty
/ –	– / –	
schol-*a*r	sch*o*-**las**-tic	

UNIT THIRTY-SEVEN
SENTENCE STRESS

Introducing the Patterns

When several words are spoken together in a phrase or sentence, certain words are stressed and others are spoken more softly and quickly.

Stressed Words

Four types of words are stressed in a sentence or phrase. Say them a little louder than the unstressed words. Following are examples of sentences containing only stressed words.

1. Most <u>content</u> words—nouns, verbs, adjectives, and adverbs.

Listen to the following examples of sentences formed with only content words. Repeat each sentence, imitating the speaker's stress pattern.

EXAMPLES

> Charles Jones taught English.
> Shirley reads aloud every day.
> Aunt Janet always makes long-distance calls.
> Jason plays basketball.

2. Interrogative words—<u>who</u>, <u>whose</u>, <u>when</u>, <u>where</u>, <u>why</u>, <u>what</u>, and <u>how</u>—when they begin questions.

Repeat these examples after the speaker.

EXAMPLES

> Where's Mary's school?
> Why's Charlie leaving?
> When's Sally's party?
> Who's coming?

168

3. Demonstrative pronouns—<u>this</u>, <u>that</u>, <u>these</u>, and <u>those</u>—when not followed by a noun.

Listen to the next examples and repeat the examples after the speaker.

EXAMPLES

What's this?	Why *a*re these here?
That's Jess*ica*'s ball.	We want*e*d those.

4. Possessive pronouns—<u>mine</u>, <u>yours</u>, <u>his</u>, <u>hers</u>, <u>ours</u>, <u>theirs</u>.

Listen to the following examples and repeat them after the speaker.

EXAMPLES

That tick*e*t's mine.	Dav*i*d sold his.
This *is* yours.	We bought ours yest*e*rday.
Barb*ara* got hers.	They gave theirs *a*way.

Unstressed Words

There is no stress on most function words in a phrase or sentence. Here, you will find these words broken down into 13 groups. Say them quickly, but be sure to pronounce the consonants clearly. The unstressed words are printed in ***italics***.

Do not stress:

1. The articles <u>a</u>, <u>an</u>, <u>the</u>.

Listen to your CD and repeat these examples after the speaker, trying to imitate the speaker's stress pattern.

EXAMPLES

a dog	*an* apple	*the* chair

2. Prepositions, such as <u>to</u>, <u>from</u>, <u>with</u>, <u>in</u>, <u>on</u>, <u>through</u>, <u>for</u>, <u>by</u>, <u>over</u>, <u>under</u>, etc.

Repeat the following examples after the speaker.

EXAMPLES

for a dog	*to the* hospital
with an apple	*around the* room
on the chair	*over the* hill
in the house	*after the* concert
through the door	*before the* show
of a family	

3. The subject pronouns <u>I</u>, <u>you</u>, <u>he</u>, <u>she</u>, <u>it</u>, <u>we</u>, and <u>they</u>.

Repeat these examples after the speaker.

EXAMPLES

I know *the* lesson.
You found *the* book *on the* shelf.
She tells secrets *to* everybody.
He talks *on the* phone too much.
We eat fish *on* Fridays.
They travel *to* Europe *a* lot.

4. The possessive pronouns <u>my</u>, <u>your</u>, <u>his</u>, <u>her</u>, <u>our</u>, <u>their</u>.

Repeat these examples after the speaker.

EXAMPLES

my car	*her* dress	*our* house
your friend	*his* brother	*their* camera

5. The object pronouns <u>me</u>, <u>you</u>, <u>her</u>, <u>him</u>, <u>us</u>, <u>them</u>.

Repeat the following examples after the speaker.

EXAMPLES

I saw *him*.	They warned *you*.
They told *me*.	*My* dad helped *us*.
We asked *her*.	Put *them on the* table.

6. The demonstrative adjectives—<u>this</u>, <u>that</u>, <u>these</u>, and <u>those</u>—when followed by a noun.

Repeat the next examples after the speaker.

EXAMPLES

This book *is* interesting.
She bought *that* house.
We like *these* shoes.
Those boys talk too loud.

7. Forms of the verb <u>be</u>—<u>am</u>, <u>are</u>, <u>is</u>, <u>was</u>, <u>were</u>, <u>aren't</u>, <u>isn't</u>, <u>wasn't</u>, <u>weren't</u>.

Say the following examples after the speaker.

EXAMPLES

I *am* here.	We *were in the* garden.
He *is a* tall man.	He *wasn't* late.
They *are* all sick.	

8. The expressions <u>there is</u> and <u>there are</u>.

Repeat the examples after the speaker.

EXAMPLES

There is a car *in the* driveway.
There is one apple *in the* basket.
There is jewelry *in* that box.
There are too many cars *on the* road.
There are five people *in the* family.

9. The <u>to</u> before a verb.

Say the following examples after the speaker.

> *He* needs *to* work.
> *I* like *to* eat early.
> *My* mother loves *to* cook.
> *We* want *to* see *the* whole movie.

10. Auxiliary verbs, such as <u>am</u>, <u>is</u>, <u>are</u>, <u>was</u>, <u>were</u>, <u>do</u>, <u>does</u>, <u>did</u>, <u>have</u>, <u>has</u>, <u>had</u>, <u>isn't</u>, <u>wasn't</u>, <u>didn't</u>, etc.

Listen to the following examples and repeat them after the speaker.

> I *am* working *in the* house.
> She *is* talking *on the* phone.
> He *was* helping *them.*
> When *do* we start school?
> Why *does* he travel so much?
> *Have* you done *your* work?
> We *have been* working all day.
> He *had* always told *the* truth.
> They *had* had *a* bad day.

11. Modal auxiliaries, such as <u>can</u>, <u>must</u>, <u>have to</u>, <u>should</u>, <u>could</u>, <u>would</u>, etc.

Repeat these examples after the speaker.

EXAMPLES

> John *can* come.
> Joe *has to* work.
> Sam *should* leave.
> We *would like to* help.
> You *mustn't* go *in the* street.
> Kathy *doesn't have to* work.

12. <u>Who</u>, <u>whose</u>, <u>when</u>, <u>where</u>, <u>why</u>, <u>what</u>, and <u>how</u> in the middle of a sentence.

Listen to these examples and repeat them after the speaker.

EXAMPLES

> Jenny has *a* cousin *whose* name *is* Smith.
> *Do you* know *where she* lives?
> Only Courtney knows *why she* said that.
> *He didn't* tell *me when to* come.
> *I can* figure out *how to* do *it.*

13. Other short function words, such as <u>and</u>, <u>but</u>, <u>or</u>, <u>so</u>, <u>not</u>, <u>if</u>, <u>as</u>, <u>because</u>, <u>whether</u>, <u>since</u>, <u>until</u>, <u>though</u>, <u>although</u>.

Repeat the following examples after the speaker.

EXAMPLES

> Mary *and* Bob have plenty *of* food, *such as* sandwiches, cakes, *and* cookies.
> Joe, *not* John, *has been* here *since* noon.
> Scott *was* worried *because his* wife *was so* late.
> I'll stay *until he* calls, *then I'll* leave *so you can* study.
> *Although you're* sick, *you can* eat *with* Carolyn *or* Sue.
> I *don't* know *whether he was* late *or* not.
> *If you* eat that much, *you'll be as* sick *as a* dog.

Exceptions

- The negative modal, <u>can't</u>, is usually stressed.

- When auxiliary verbs and modal auxiliaries are not followed by a verb, they have strong stress.

Listen to the following examples and repeat them after the speaker.

EXAMPLES

She can't help *him with the* cooking.
I'll come *to the* party *if I* can.
We would lend *you the* car *if we* could.
Carol has *a* new car, *but* Margaret doesn't.
He doesn't know *I'm* unhappy, *but* I am.

Practice for Mastery

Now practice the stress patterns discussed in this unit by repeating the following sentences after the speaker.

CD 4
TRACK
5

EXAMPLES

The money *is in the* bank.
He came over *to* talk *to me.*
She can help *him with the* cooking.
I should buy *a* new dress *for the* wedding.
We could lend *you our* car.
I will send *you a* letter tomorrow.
They're walking *to the* store.
He didn't work *because he was* sick.
Karen *and* Danny stayed *until they* knew *whether or not*
Val *was* coming.

- Any word can be given extra stress to emphasize or clarify a statement.

In the examples that follow, emphasis is shown in boldface. Listen, and repeat each sentence after the speaker.

Examples

	Meaning
I wanted to go to the **circus**.	(not the **movies**.)
They didn't go to **France**.	(They went to Paris, **Virginia**!)
I lost my ring on my way **to** the store.	(not **from** the store.)
He gave her the money.	(**I** didn't give her the money.)
He **gave** her the money.	(He didn't **lend** her the money.)
He gave **her** the money.	(He didn't give the money to **me**.)
He gave her the **money**.	(He didn't give her the **car**.)

Be careful not to use extra stress if you do not intend special meaning.

Next, listen to the following paragraph, paying close attention to the stress patterns.

Learning to speak a language is a little like learning to dance. They both take a long time to master, but are fun from the beginning. Both require interaction with another person, who is saying or doing something different. Fluent speakers and good dancers don't have to think about their skills. They perform them naturally. To acquire these skills, you need a lot of practice and patience. Encouragement from someone else helps a great deal.

Now, repeat the paragraph, one phrase at a time, after the speaker.

Learning *to* speak
a language
is a little *like*
learning *to* dance.
They both take *a* long time
to master,
but are fun
from the beginning.
Both require interaction
with another person,
who is saying *or* doing
something different.
Fluent speakers
and good dancers
don't have to think
about their skills.
They perform *them* naturally.
To acquire *these* skills,
you need *a* lot *of* practice
and patience.
Encouragement *from* someone else
helps *a* great deal.

Read the paragraph aloud again, practicing the proper stress. Try recording your reading on tape to see if it sounds natural.

Here is another paragraph. Listen to it on your tape, noting the speaker's stress patterns.

Last May we had a surprise party at my house for one of my friends. It was his fiftieth birthday. We invited about thirty people, and most of them were able to come. One couple even traveled all the way from New Jersey. Several people who had been away for a long time were here. Most of the guests hadn't met each other before the party, but they were having a wonderful time talking during the

half-hour before the birthday man arrived. It seemed that
a very special person was a magnet for other special people. When he got here, he was really surprised, and happy
to see so many friends. It was a good party.

Now, repeat each phrase after the speaker.

Last May
we had *a* surprise party
at my house
for one *of my* friends.
It was his fiftieth birthday.
We invited *about* thirty people,
and most *of them*
were able *to* come.
One couple *even* traveled
all *the* way *from* New Jersey.
Several people
who had been away
for a long time
were here.
Most *of the* guests
hadn't met each other
before the party,
but they were having
a wonderful time talking
during the half-hour
before the birthday man arrived.
It seemed
that a very special person
was a magnet
for other special people.
When he got here,
he was really surprised,
and happy *to* see
so many friends.
It was a good party.

Read the paragraph aloud again, comparing your stresses
with those of the speaker.

PART FOUR
INTONATION
PATTERNS

Intonation is the "musical score" of a language. Each "tune" has a special meaning. In the following units, the intonation patterns are represented graphically: A horizontal line means that the words are all delivered at approximately the same pitch level; a rising line means that the pitch rises; a descending line means that it falls.

Unit Thirty-Eight
Greetings

Pattern ___⌐.

On your CD, listen to the intonation pattern in the following examples, and repeat them after the speaker.

EXAMPLES

Good morning.	Be careful.
Good afternoon.	Drive safely.
Good evening.	Say hello to your mother.
Good night.	Goodbye.
Hello.	Bye.
Hi.	Thank you.
Excuse me.	You're welcome.
Take care.	See you later.

When you say the name of the person you are talking to, add a second pattern to the previous greeting: ___/.

Now, repeat these phrases.

EXAMPLES

Good morning, Bill.
Good evening, Miss Jones.
Be careful, Emily.
Say hello to your mother, John.

UNIT THIRTY-NINE
STATEMENTS

Introducing the Patterns

Pattern 1: ⎯⋀.

Listen to the speaker's intonation pattern in the following examples of one-phrase sentences, then repeat each sentence after the speaker.

EXAMPLES

She's my sister.	I have a dog.
They're from Venezuela.	It's beautiful.
We're going to visit them.	We love it.
He's here.	

Pattern 2: ⎯ ⎯⋀.

Listen to the following examples of two-phrase sentences, and repeat them after the speaker.

EXAMPLES

He's here, but she isn't.
I have a dog, and you have a cat.
She's my sister, and he's my cousin.
When I see him, I'll tell him.
After you get here, have a cup of coffee.
Before you start, take a deep breath.

UNIT FORTY
QUESTIONS

Introducing the Patterns

Pattern 1: Tag Questions _⁀_⁄?

This is the same pattern used for a greeting followed by a name. (See Unit Thirty-eight.)

Listen to and repeat each of the following sentences after the speaker.

EXAMPLES

> He's coming, isn't he?
> You're a lawyer, aren't you?
> My sister told you, didn't she?
> You'll come to my party, won't you?

Pattern 2: Tag Questions Indicating Displeasure _⁀_⁀?

A message of displeasure can be conveyed through a different intonation pattern. Listen to the same sentences, noting the change in the speaker's tone and repeat each question after the speaker.

EXAMPLES

> He's coming, isn't he?
> You're a lawyer, aren't you?
> My sister told you, didn't she?
> You'll come to my party, won't you?

This pattern can also indicate confidence in the response.

As before, repeat the example.

EXAMPLES

> The water's nice, isn't it?

Pattern 3: Questions with Question Words ⌄?

You will note that this is the same pattern as that used in greetings and one-phrase statements. Try to imitate the speaker's tone.

Listen to and repeat each sentence after the speaker.

EXAMPLES

When are you going?	Why are you crying?
Who is the teacher?	Where did he go?

When an answer to your question is suggested, it is on a higher tone: ⌄ ⟋

As before, repeat these examples after the speaker.

EXAMPLES

When are you going, Friday?
Who is the teacher, Miss Smith?
Why are you crying, to make me feel bad?
Where did he go, to the movies?

The answers to the preceding questions have their own pattern: ⌐\. (pause) ⌐\.

Repeat these examples after the speaker.

EXAMPLES

Yes. Friday.	No. I can't help it.
No. Miss Jones.	Yes. To the movies.

Pattern 4: Questions Indicating Annoyance ⌐?

Next, repeat these questions that show annoyance through the intonation pattern.

EXAMPLES

> Why do you ask?
> When is he coming?
> Where did you hear that?
> Who did this to you?

Pattern 5: Questions Without Question Words ___↗?

Here is the last set of questions. As before, repeat each one after the speaker.

EXAMPLES

Are you happy?	Was she there?
Will he win?	Were they hurt?
Do you like it?	Did you see it?

Unit Forty-One
Counting and Listing

Introducing the Patterns

Fundamentally, the intonation pattern used in counting and listing is a series of level and rising tones that end with a final drop in pitch.

Counting

Listen to your CD and repeat the following examples after the speaker.

EXAMPLES

> One, two, three, four, five.
>
> Four hundred and thirty-seven, four hundred and thirty-eight,
>
> four hundred and thirty-nine, four hundred and forty.

Listing

As before, repeat these examples after the speaker.

EXAMPLES

> I need shoes, socks, shirts, and pants.
>
> He ate two hamburgers, french fries, and an ice cream cone.
>
> She likes perfume, chocolates, flowers, and money.

Unit Forty-Two
Options

Introducing the Patterns

Pattern 1: When the Question Requires a "Yes" or "No" Answer

Listen to your CD and repeat the questions after the speaker. Then listen for and repeat the answers.

EXAMPLES

Questions	Answers
Would you like potatoes or carrots?	No, I would rather have fruit.
Are you unhappy or uncomfortable?	No, I feel just fine.
Will he eat ice cream or cake?	Yes, he probably will (but he should be on a diet).
Would you like a drink or something?	Yes, please, I'm thirsty.

Pattern 2: When the Question Offers a Limited Choice

EXAMPLES

Questions	Answers
Would you like potatoes or carrots?	I would like carrots.
Are you unhappy or uncomfortable?	I'm unhappy.
Will he eat ice cream or cake?	He'll have cake.

Practice in Context

Listen to the following dialogues on your CD and repeat each line after the speaker.

CD 4
TRACK
11

1. — Can you help me with these boxes, Steve?
   — No. I can't.
   — Why not?
   — They're too heavy. I hurt my back and I'm not supposed to lift anything heavy.
   — Well . . . how am I going to get them upstairs?
   — Call John and see if he'll help you!

2. — Hi, Carol. How are you?
   — Fine, thanks. How are you Ms. Johnson?
   — Fine. How's school these days?
   — Oh . . . it's O.K. but we have too much homework!
   — Are you going to the game?
   — Yes, are you?
   — No. I have to clean the garage.
   — O.K. . . . see you later.
   — Bye, drive carefully!

3. — Where are you going, Mom?
   — To the movies. Do you want to come?
   — Oh . . . I'd love to, but I have to go to the library.
   — The library! Wow! I'm really proud of you. Are you doing research?
   — No . . . I'm going to pick up my friends. They need a ride home.

4. — Come live with me in the city. You'll have lots of fun.
   — I don't like the city. It's too noisy. There's too much traffic and pollution, and there's no place to park. Why don't you come live with me in the country?
   — I hate the country. It's too far away, and there's more traffic out there than in the city. Besides, there's nothing to do there. Don't you get bored?
   — You're looking for an argument, aren't you? I can see we weren't meant for each other.
   — Don't be silly! I think this is a perfect relationship. I really like living alone.

Appendix

1. More Words to Practice

/ə/ in first syllable:	/ɪ/	/u/
*a*bout	did	bush
*a*bove	fig	cush*io*n
*a*dore	gin	pudding
*a*gain	his	cook
*a*head	kids	good
*a*jar	lip	hood
*a*llow	live	rook
*a*lone	pin	stood
*a*nnoy	sist*e*r	wool
*a*ppear	tin	wood
*a*round	win	would
*a*way	zip	should
*e*lect	building	
*e*merge	guild	
*e*nough	guilty	
*e*ssent*ia*l	quick	
*e*xact	quilt	
*e*xactly	cymb*a*l	
*o*bject	hymn	
*o*ccas*io*n	nymph	
*o*ffend		

CD 4 TRACK 13

/iy/

need
seed
deep
keep
creep
squeeze
extreme
machine
squeal
lead
leap
please
tease
clean
floppy
silly
lovely
friendly

/uw/

mood
boo hoo
coo
goose
moon
noon
soon
zoo
whose
drew
grew
Jew
jewel
jewelry
stew
clue
glue
true
junior
truce
tune

/iuw/

pew
hew
Hugh
unity
universe
university
useful
usual
utility
fume
huge
municipal
mute
puny

CD 4 TRACK 14

/ʌ/

*a*bove
dove
shove
ton
won
bun
fun
stuff
sun
ugh
tough

/ɛ/

beg
bend
crept
leg
lend
mend
regret
rest
send
leapt
plea*su*re
ready
stead
tread
jeop*a*rdy

/ow/

no
so
loan
loaf
grown
shown
known
stone
phone
bould*e*r
although
dough
grow
blow
show
tow
mow
b*e*low
Joe
foe
toe

/owr/	/oiy/
bore	coin
gore	Demoines
more	groin
store	join
tore	loin
dork	boy
fork	destroy
forty	enjoy
north	joy
short	ploy
worn	soy
boor	toy
floor	
poor	
quart	
wart	
court	
hoard	
roar	

CD 4
TRACK
15

/eə/

jam
can
fan
land
pan
ran
van
hand
stand
care
dare
fare
glare
pare
stare
fair
hair
pair
bear
tear
wear

/eiy/

crate	refrain
crave	remain
fate	stain
frame	train
grape	grey
lame	hey
late	prey
plane	whey
same	buffet
save	fillet
state	persuade
tame	feign
tape	freight
staple	neigh
clay	reign
fray	weigh
gray	weight
May	great
play	
pray	
stay	
cafe	
resumé	
gain	
grain	
plain	

CD 4 TRACK 16

/ɔ/

gone
belong
long
prong
song
wrong
call
fall
mall
tall
wall
auction
caucus
daunt
gaunt
haunted
jaundice
jaunt
jaunty
pause
raucous
taut
caught
fraught
haughty

/ɔ/ (cont'd.)	/ae/
taught	black
bawdy	brat
crawl	cap
dawdle	castle
flaw	crack
jaw	dad
lawn	dagger
raw	dapper
saw	fasten
tawny	flag
bought	flap
brought	flat
fought	gag
sought	gash
thought	hash
wrought	hat
broad	jack
	lack
	lap
	map
	nap
	pack
	quack
	rack
	racquet
	sack
	sash
	slash
	stack
	tack
	trash

CD 4
TRACK
17

/aəow/

bower
brown
clown
cow
flower
frown
howl
jowl
now
owl
plow
prowl
shower
tower
town
vowel
wow
dour
flour
gouge
loud
mouse
mouth
our

/a/	/ar/	/aiy/
father	bar	bride
garage	barn	fire
ha ha	car	hire
Hawaii	carbs	I'm
wad	carve	I've
wash	dark	invite
watch	far	kind
yacht	farmer	quite
bother	farther	trite
clock	jar	twice
crop	lard	denied
flop	park	dried
mop	star	fried
office	starve	tie
plot	tar	tried
stock		blight
stop		flight
top		might
entree		plight
ennui		sigh
		slight
		haiku
		height
		cry
		cypress
		fry
		my
		buyer
		dye
		lye

CD 4
TRACK
18

2. Pronunciation differences when the letter <u>e</u> is added to a one-syllable word

/ɪ/	/aiy/	/aə/	/eiy/
bid	bide	bad	bade
hid	hide	mad	made
rid	ride	cam	came
Sid	side	dam	dame
dim	dime	gam	game
Tim	time	lam	lame
din	dine	Sam	same
fin	fine	tam	tame
pin	pine	ban	bane
win	wine	can	cane
grip	gripe	Dan	Dane
pip	pipe	pan	pane
rip	ripe		
trip	tripe		

/ae/	/eiy/
fad	fade
lad	lade
gap	gape
rap	rape
cat	Cate
hat	hate
mat	mate
Nat	Nate
rat	rate

CD 4 TRACK 20

/a/	/eə/
bar	bare
car	care
far	fare
mar	mare
par	pare
star	stare
tar	tare

/a/	/eiy/
wad	wade

/a/	/ow/
rob	robe
cod	code
mod	mode
nod	node
rod	rode
Tom	tome
cop	cope
hop	hope
mop	mope
slop	slope
dot	dote
not	note
tot	tote

/ɛ/	/iy/
met	mete
pet	Pete

/ʌ/	/uw/
rub	rube
tub	tube
dud	dude
dun	dune

/ʌ/	/iuw/
cut	cute

CD1

Track

1 Introduction
2 Unit 1 The Sound /ə/
3 Unit 2 The Sound /ɪ/
4 Unit 3 The Sound /u/
5 Unit 4 The Sound /iy/
6 Unit 5 The Sound /uw/
7 Unit 6 The Sound /iuw/
8 Unit 7 The Sound /ʌ/
9 Unit 8 The Sound /ɛ/
10 Unit 9 The Sound /ow/
11 Unit 10 The Sound /oiy/
12 Unit 11 The Sound /eə/
13 Unit 12 The Sound /eiy/
14 Unit 13 The Sound /ɔ/
15 Unit 14 The Sound /æ/
16 Unit 15 The Sound /æow/
17 Unit 16 The Sound /a/

CD2

Track

1 Unit 17 The Sound /aiy/
2 Unit 18 The Sounds /p/, /b/
3 Unit 19 The Sounds /t/, /d/
4 Introducing the Sound /d/
5 Unit 20 The Sounds /k/, /g/
6 Introducing the Sound /g/
7 Unit 21 The Sounds /f/, /v/
8 Unit 22 The Sounds /ch/, /j/
9 Unit 23 The Sounds /sh/, /zh/
10 Unit 24 The Sounds /s/, /z/
11 Introducing the Sound /z/

CD3

Track

1 Unit 25 The Sounds /l/, /r/
2 Unit 26 The Sounds /m/, /n/, /ŋ/
3 Introducing the Sound /ŋ/
4 Unit 27 The Sounds /θ/, /ð/
5 Unit 28 The Sound /h/
6 Unit 29 The Sounds /w/, /y/
7 Unit 30 Double Consonants
8 Unit 31 Syllables and Stress
9 Unit 32 Two-Syllable Words
10 Introducing Secondary Stress
11 Unit 33 Words with Three or
More Syllables

CD4

Track

1 Unit 34 One-Syllable Prefixes
2 Unit 35 Two-Syllable Prefixes
3 Unit 36 Suffixes
4 Unit 37 Sentence Stress
5 Practice for Mastery
6 Unit 38 Greetings
7 Unit 39 Statements
8 Unit 40 Questions
9 Unit 41 Counting and Listing
10 Unit 42 Options
11 Practice in Context
12–20 Appendix

4R9
᷍7-7160

(#153) R9/12